SPEAKING THE TRUTH IN LOVE

Education, Mission, and Witness in Contemporary Orthodoxy

THOMAS HOPKO

Speaking the Truth in LOVE

Education, Mission, and Witness
in Contemporary Orthodoxy

ST VLADIMIR'S SEMINARY PRESS
CRESTWOOD, NEW YORK
2004

Library of Congress Cataloging-in-Publication Data

Hopko, Thomas.
  Speaking the truth in love : education, mission, and witness in
contemporary Orthodoxy / Thomas Hopko.—1st American pbk. ed.
    p. cm.
  ISBN 0–88141–263–5 (pbk.)
  1. Orthodox Eastern Church. I. Title.
  BX325.H67 2004
  281.9—dc22

                                                        2004010478

ST VLADIMIR'S SEMINARY PRESS
575 Scarsdale Road, Crestwood, NY 10707
1-800-204-2665
www.svspress.com

ISBN 0-88141-263-5

PRINTED IN THE UNITED STATES OF AMERICA

Contents

Introduction

These addresses and talks were mostly written during my decade as dean of St. Vladimir's Seminary from 1992 to 2002. I treat my subjects in each of them within the conditions of contemporary Orthodoxy, particularly in North America. I reflect on education and spiritual formation in Orthodox theological schools, on preaching and teaching in the church community, on missionary and philanthropic activity, on the relationship between clergy and laity, and on the work of Christian men and women in church and society.

These reflections are, in a sense, all about the same thing, each put in a different way for a different purpose. Read as a whole, they are meant to provide insight and encouragement about what it means for Christians to speak and do God's truth in love by the Holy Spirit's power in our present world.

The book's title comes from St Paul's letter to the Ephesians. The essays are all about this extraordinary passage:

> There is one body and one Spirit, just as you were called to the one hope that belongs to your call, one Lord, one faith, one baptism, one God and Father of us all, who is above all and through all and in all.
>
> But grace was given to each of us according to the measure of Christ's gift. Therefore it is said, "When he ascended on high he led a host of captives and he gave gifts to men." . . . He who descended is he who also ascended far above all the heavens, that he might fill all things.
>
> And his gifts were that some should be apostles, some prophets, some evangelists, some pastors and teachers, to equip the saints for the work of ministry, for building up the body of Christ until we all attain to the unity of the faith and of the knowledge of the Son of God, to perfect humanity, to the measure of the stature of the fullness of Christ; so that we may no longer be children tossed to and fro and carried about with every wind of doctrine, by human cunning, by craftiness in deceitful wiles.
>
> Rather, speaking the truth in love, we are to grow up in every way into him who is the head, into Christ, from whom the whole body,

joined and knit together by every joint with which it is supplied, when each part is working properly, makes bodily growth and upbuilds itself in love. (Eph 4.4–8, 10–16)

"Speaking the truth in love," *alitheuontes en agapi*, may also possibly be rendered *doing the truth in love* or *speaking and acting truthfully in love*, since the biblical Hebrew word for "Word," *de'var*, means not only speech and thought, but also act and thing. The "Word of the Lord," *de'var YHWH* or *logos kyriou*, is not only spoken and proclaimed, it is done and enacted. The Christian faith teaches that God's Word may not be spoken by people, and indeed cannot be, unless it is also obeyed and practiced.

These essays call for a strict order and discipline in Christian education, mission, and witness. The gospel, and the order and discipline of thought and behavior that the gospel demands, are revealed in the Bible as a whole. Therefore all Christian activities are rooted and grounded in the crucified Christ as he is presented in the canonical Scriptures. Holy tradition is understood as the ongoing sacramental and spiritual life of the Church within which the Bible is read, heard, prayed, and practiced by believing Christians. Tradition is also the interpretation and application of God's biblical Word for believers as this living Word is understood, explained, and enacted in the Church's liturgical worship, dogmatic teaching, canonical order, and spiritual life witnessed by the saints. Consequently, I believe Orthodox Christians must read and hear the Bible critically within the tradition of the Church, which includes being informed and illumined by all relevant scholarship—especially historical, literary, linguistic, cultural, and archeological studies.

All the essays in this collection are based on my conviction that Orthodoxy, rightly understood and lived, is God's gospel in Jesus Christ that is the saving truth for all people. I am convinced of this, despite the personal sins of Orthodox people and the institutional sins of Orthodox churches in a world that becomes increasingly complicated, confused, and corrupt. Contemporary Western culture has been in the process of deterioration since before the founding of the United States and is now largely characterized by its conscious opposition to traditional Christianity as understood by Orthodoxy. Orthodox Christians in America must, after honest assessment and in good conscience, accept this situation courageously as their own and take responsibility for it before God and their neighbors.

These essays also all affirm that God's truth, wisdom, light, and love are found among Christians in heterodox churches and among people of non-Christian convictions and views. It is my belief that Orthodox Christians should thankfully affirm and rejoice in the graces of God and the vestiges of the Church that truly exist in other faith communities. Likewise, Orthodox Christians must address the errors and sins that they see in others with gentleness and respect, as they struggle to witness to divine truth, goodness, and beauty in human being and life.

Orthodox Christians also have the obligation to advocate before the face of God for all creatures and the whole of creation. They must identify with all people and take up their sins and burdens as God in Christ has taken up their own. They must also apply the standards of judgment found in Christ's gospel equally to Orthodox and non-Orthodox alike—even rendering stricter judgment upon themselves and holding themselves to greater accountability, in accordance with the Scriptures and writings of the saints, given what they claim to have received in Christ and his Church. Further, Orthodox Christians may defend their convictions only by witnessing to Christ's truth and love through sacrificial service to everyone, without exception or condition. Such witness and service are never accomplished without suffering.

Finally, I pray that these essays will be received as benevolent attempts to speak the truth in love.

Protopresbyter Thomas Hopko
Dean Emeritus
St Vladimir's Orthodox Theological Seminary
Pascha 2004

Theological Education at St Vladimir's Seminary[1]

S t Vladimir's is a theological seminary educating men and women for service in the Orthodox Church. Most of its students are preparing for pastoral work in the ordained ministries, primarily in North America. Others are preparing for academic and scholarly service. And others are studying to become missionaries, religious educators, chaplains, pastoral counselors, writers, church musicians, iconographers, and monastics.

As an Orthodox theological seminary, St Vladimir's situates its curriculum of scholarly studies and practical training in the context of liturgical worship and spiritual formation. Developing each of these areas—the academic, the practical, and the spiritual—and maintaining the right relationship among them, provide the school's dean, faculty, and trustees with countless demands for decisions and actions.

The dean's task, as the person charged with overseeing the life and work of the school, is to assure that decisions are made and actions are taken in a setting where all members of the community are properly included. The dean's duty is to see that all questions and suggestions are received and considered, all differences and distinctions are cherished and respected, and all structures and procedures are defined and followed. The dean is called to lead an educational community where everyone is encouraged and empowered to listen, to speak, and to act in a collegial and conciliar manner, which necessarily requires compromise and consensus.

Academic Education

St Vladimir's seeks to provide its students with an education in the classical fields of Orthodox Church studies: scripture and liturgy,

[1]This address was given at Fr Thomas's installation as dean of St Vladimir's Seminary in December 1992.

church history and patristics, dogmatic and practical theology, spirituality and ethics, canon law, homiletics, languages, music, and art. Finding the best way of organizing, integrating, and teaching its academic and practical subjects is a perennial problem at the seminary. Converts from diverse backgrounds and experiences, both North American and foreign, comprise half the student body. The "native" Orthodox men and women are also of diverse countries, cultures, traditions, and ecclesial experiences.[2] The heterogeneous character of the student body presents enormous pedagogical challenges at a time when the number of foreign students, especially from Eastern Europe and the former Soviet Union, increases according to the school's ability to secure funds to support their studies.

Vision in living communities always means *revision*, and organization is continual *reorganization*. St Vladimir's Seminary is no exception. Continual renewal and refinement of the seminary's curriculum of studies, with the development of more effective methods of instruction, are necessary and unavoidable. The school must be constantly changing in order to remain faithful to its unchanging mission of educating and integrating its students into the vision and life of the Orthodox Church.

Opportunities must be available for the teachers to refine their skills, deepen their knowledge, and convey their findings. We are grateful, thanks largely to the work of our advancement office, that in addition to receiving funding from foundations for trustee development, student and employee assistance, scholarships, and library expansion, the seminary has also received grants to develop its present faculty and to find future teachers for the school. The new faculty by-laws and handbook include guidelines for professional growth contracts and sabbatical leaves for the seminary's professors and teachers. The seminary press continues to provide its instructors with opportunities for publication.

---

[2]Converts, students born abroad, and the children of clergy comprise the majority of the student population in all Orthodox seminaries (and monasteries) in North America. Conversely, children born of Orthodox parents in America are not coming to study theology and to serve the Church. There are many reasons for this: Orthodox Christians who themselves experienced a relatively low standard of living raised their children to be materially successful and satisfied; young people did not understand church services because of the languages used and the manner of their celebration; they received little or no spiritual education and training at home or in the churches; they witnessed in-fighting and turmoil in their churches; and churches were concerned almost exclusively with liturgical, cultural, social, and political activities, rather than the application of spiritual truths in personal lives.

Practical Training

All seminary courses have a pastoral, missionary, and apologetic orientation. The Scriptures and services, saints and sacraments, and councils and canons that witness to the Church's vision and life are examined, interpreted, and applied in relation to contemporary issues and realities. This requires reflection on the state of things and the spirit of the times, and direct involvement with men, women, and children in today's Church and world.

The seminary's practical theology program, which includes parish assignments and fieldwork outside an ecclesiastical setting, supplies some practical training while the students are still in school. Its purpose is to begin a process of developing the students' self-knowledge and technical skills, and to provide them with experiential terms of reference for their academic studies. We look to the time when internship training and continuing education for pastors and church workers, together with programs for personal and professional counsel and nurture, will be a mandatory part of the Orthodox Church's program of theological education.

Liturgical Life and Spiritual Formation

Liturgical worship and spiritual counsel provide the context for scholarly study and practical training in an Orthodox seminary. Theology is not simply studied, say the saints, it is suffered. It is not only a matter of ink, but of blood. It requires prayer and repentance. It is an ascetic as well as an intellectual activity. It involves mind and heart, reason and will, and spirit and body. It is a vision born from action; an action informed by vision.

Prayer is the proof of theology. Spiritual growth and ethical action are its fruit. Theologians are those who truly pray, and those who truly pray are theologians. The rule of worship is the rule of faith. Theology is sung by one voice in the midst of the Church. It is the "climax of purity," an experiential knowledge of God through a communion of love born of gratitude and praise in the midst of affliction and trial.

We know very well that such traditional sayings, so often repeated in Orthodox circles, are all too often nothing more than empty words for which account will be given to God on the Day of Judgment. But the mindless mouthing of truths does not make them any less true. Liturgical and personal prayer, psalmody, hymnody, spiritual reading and listening, meditation and contemplation, confession of sins, revealing of thoughts and feelings, and sacramental participation and ascetical struggle under the guidance of elder members of the community are an essential part of Orthodox theological education.

Liturgical worship and spiritual striving, however, do not deny or diminish the need for scholarly study and scientific research. They rather demand it, for true prayer and genuine spiritual effort are rigorously respectful of reality and unconditionally committed to truth. Only persons freed from passion and prejudice are capable of achieving academic excellence and scientific insight. The Holy Spirit enables knowledge of truth not by magical power or mechanistic programming but by graciously liberating those who seek—even in scientific study and critical research—from whatever darkens, distorts, and disfigures their minds and hearts.

The seminary's goal, then, is to provide its students with liturgical worship and spiritual guidance in their most beneficial forms. Liturgical gatherings with students serving, preaching, reading, singing, composing, and conducting music develop the students' technical skills. They are part of the school's practical educational program. But the seminary chapel must always remain a place of true worship where the liturgy is celebrated and not merely performed, where the community prays and not merely practices.

Structure and Style

The structure and style of seminary life and work are of inestimable pedagogical significance. Students learn not only from lectures, liturgies, and practical training projects. They learn from how they are treated in classes and church services, and in offices, dormitories, bookstores, and homes. Their way of acceptance and entry into the school, their financial assistance and housing, their work assignments and recreation, their interaction with teachers, counselors, secretaries, advancement officers, salespersons, cooks, and groundskeepers all contribute to their theological education and spiritual formation.

Students observe how things in the seminary are organized and operate. They watch how people behave, how money is raised and spent, how resources are used, how priorities and interests are determined and expressed, and how people are treated. Their attitudes and actions, including their relation to their studies and spiritual life while still in school, are shaped by these observations. They live with these experiences for the rest of their lives.

Integrity and Maturity

The seminary's mission to share significantly in educating church workers who are theologically sound, intellectually capable, spiritually mature, and pastorally engaged is part of a larger task which begins before the students arrive on campus and continues long after they leave. The seminary, with the Church as a whole, must understand the crucial, yet strictly limited role of a two, three or four-year educational program in a theological school. Seminary education has to be the best that the Church has to offer, but it cannot be everything. The seminary must not be expected to do things beyond its capability and competence.

The most important thing that the seminary must accomplish, the absence of which indicates tragic failure, is to teach its teachable students the difference between what is essential and nonessential in Orthodox Church teaching and practice. The school must distinguish by word and deed what is truly of God and what is simply from human beings. The seminary must display the diversity and affirm the variety of thought and expression that God's Holy Spirit inspires within the Body of Christ. It must also disclose its depth and complexity. Better real darkness than false light, say the saints; better real confusion than false clarity. Oversimplification, exaggeration, reduction, distortion, and caricature are abiding temptations for those engaged in theological studies.

The fears and anxieties of our time, the search for safety and security, the explosion of information about all aspects of Orthodoxy after centuries of widespread ignorance and misinformation, and the emergence of self-taught theologians and self-appointed elders have resulted in misconceptions and errors about Orthodox Christianity which produce suspicions, accusations, and divisions among Orthodox Christians, and between Orthodox Christians and those outside the Orthodox tradition.

St Vladimir's Seminary is called, with all Orthodox theological schools, to bring sobriety and sanity to church life and activity. It is called to be a place of balance and measure, of soundness and stability, of openness and honesty, of freedom and responsibility. The seminary must protect those who insist on the highest standards of academic excellence from accusations of indifference to spiritual formation and pastoral training and application. It must also defend those who stress the necessity for liturgical worship and ascetical life from being denigrated for allegedly denying the need for scholarship and pastoral service. It must shelter those who emphasize pastoral sensibility and the development of practical skills from charges of downplaying academic excellence, liturgical worship, and spiritual striving. The seminary must be a place where those who stress fidelity to Orthodox tradition are not charged with being closed-minded and "dogmatistic" where those involved in critical studies are not labeled liberal and modernistic, where those faithful to the Church's canonical norms and rules of worship are not slandered as being legalistic and rubric-oriented. It must be a community of those who rejoice with gratitude in what is good, true, and beautiful outside the Church's canonical bounds, knowing that their devotion to Christ and the Church is not thereby put in question. It must be an institution where those working for cooperation and unity among Christians, and indeed among all human beings, within and without formal ecumenical organizations and movements, know that they are not viewed as betrayers of Orthodoxy because they dedicate their lives to the reconciliation and reunion of divided people created in God's image and likeness.

Men and women who are truly theologically and spiritually educated reveal a boldness born of humility, a confidence tempered by tentativeness, a speech generated by silence, an apology inspired by charity. They resist premature closure of complex issues and superficial answers to complicated questions. They know how to live with ambiguity as they give, with meekness and gentleness, account for the hope that is in them. They speak the truth in love with an enlightened zeal that prevents them from replacing God's righteousness with a righteousness of their own. They evangelize without seeking to convert. They witness without seeking to win. They teach without desiring to dominate. They testify to truths in which they delight and find life, whatever the cost of their convictions, because they simply cannot do otherwise. And they have infinite respect for everyone and everything.

The mission of St Vladimir's Seminary is to contribute to educating such humble, free, and fearless men and women for service in the Orthodox Church. The seminary dean, faculty, trustees, and staff can hardly be expected to be wholly successful in accomplishing this awesome task. They are expected, however, to be faithfully committed to its most fruitful fulfillment.

Honorary Doctorate for
Ecumenical Patriarch Bartholomew[1]

We thank God for enabling His All Holiness Patriarch Bartholomew to be with us today. We are honored that he has chosen to bestow his patriarchal blessings on our theological school.

We know, by his words and the witness of his life, that Patriarch Bartholomew steadfastly supports the work of theological education, especially graduate theological study, which insures sound education on all levels of church life and contributes to all aspects of the Church's saving mission.

Patriarch Bartholomew sacrificed much of his life to learn many languages and to be educated at the highest academic level. He made this sacrifice to prepare himself to serve God, the Church, his country, and humanity to the best of his abilities and in accordance with his gifts. Having attained the highest position of archiepiscopal leadership in his own church and, therefore, in the entire Orthodox Church throughout the world, His All Holiness continues to affirm and support higher theological education, as his presence with us today clearly shows.

The patriarch's special desire, for which fulfillment good-willed people everywhere are working and praying, is the immediate reopening of the Patriarchal Theological School of Halki, his alma mater where he once served as assistant dean, so that this venerable institution might once again take its rightful place among the preeminent theological faculties of the world.

The words and witness of His All Holiness Patriarch Bartholomew over many years wonderfully demonstrate the Christian conviction—which is shared by all who fear God and love humanity—that knowledge

[1]St Vladimir's Orthodox Theological Seminary awarded a Doctor of Divinity *honoris causa* to Ecumenical Patriarch Bartholomew of Constantinople in October 1997. Fr Thomas Hopko gave this address in honor of that occasion.

for its own sake is curiosity, and knowledge for one's own sake is vanity, while knowledge for the sake of others is charity.

The visit of His All Holiness to St Vladimir's Seminary as Archbishop of Constantinople, New Rome, and Ecumenical Patriarch, also clearly demonstrates that Patriarch Bartholomew's personal theological education and academic learning, together with his entire spiritual formation in the Church from his earliest childhood, has truly blossomed into a ministry of all-embracing charity as befits his duty to "preside in love" among his brother bishops within Christ's holy Church.

The patriarch's support of St Vladimir's Seminary, as a member of the advisory board of its capital campaign[2] and in his many acts of kindness, such as that which we are now cherishing, is most gratifying. The patriarch's coming to St Vladimir's today not only affirms the work of this school but also serves as a recognition of the work of Orthodox theological education in North America, from the Alaskan mission at the end of the eighteenth century to the present day. St Vladimir's Seminary (together with St Tikhon's, both founded in 1938, a year after the establishment of Holy Cross Greek Orthodox School of Theology[3]) is the direct heir of the Orthodox theological seminaries that initially operated on this continent. These include the seminaries in New Archangel (now Sitka) Alaska; San Francisco, California; Minneapolis, Minnesota; and Tenafly, New Jersey, whose labors were brutally interrupted by the Bolshevik revolution in Russia.

In honoring our school with his presence today, His All Holiness honors two centuries of sacrificial service in the field of Orthodox theological education in North America. He raises his hands in blessing over the efforts of thousands of faithful teachers, students, and supporters of seminaries in this land. He aligns himself especially with the learned hierarchs in our seminary's history, including the canonized saints: Innocent, the great missionary in Alaska and first bishop in North America who ended his days as the Metropolitan of Moscow; Tikhon the Confessor, Archbishop of North America from 1898 to 1907 (before the days of American "jurisdictions"), who completed his earthly course as the confessing Patriarch of Moscow and who suffered

---

[2]A capital campaign was begun in 1990 for the seminary's new library, administrative offices, and married student housing.

[3]St Tikhon's Seminary and St Vladimir's Seminary are under the governance of the Orthodox Church in America. Holy Cross Seminary is under the governance of the Greek Orthodox Archdiocese of America.

under Marxist persecution; and Bishop Nikolai (Velimirovich) of Zica, the internationally renowned scholar, writer, teacher, pastor, and confessor for the faith, who possessed several earned doctoral degrees and who often visited St Vladimir's Seminary. We treasure his gift to our chapel, an icon of St Sava of Serbia, inscribed on the back with his handwritten blessing.

In recalling the history of Orthodox theological education in North America, we cannot fail to raise the name of Metropolitan Leonty. As a young priest possessing the highest theological education from the Theological Academy of Kiev, Fr Leonid Turkevich was appointed rector of the theological seminary in Minneapolis in 1906, at the request of the American Archbishop, later Russian Patriarch, St Tikhon. He served in this same position at St Platon's Seminary in Tenafly, New Jersey. After becoming bishop of Chicago following the death of his wife, he led the movement in 1938 to open a seminary at St Tikhon's Monastery in South Canaan, Pennsylvania, and a graduate school of theology (in Russian terminology, a "theological academy") in New York City. The graduate school was named for St Vladimir, Great Prince of Kiev, who, as the hymn in his honor states, "found Christ the priceless pearl" by "sending servants to Constantinople for the Orthodox faith." St Vladimir was chosen as the patron of the school since 1938 was the nine hundred and fiftieth anniversary of the enlightenment of the people of Rus, who were baptized by the great prince in 988. The name of St Vladimir was selected to emphasize the missionary character of the Church and seminary in North America. Metropolitan Leonty also served as rector of St Vladimir's after the first dean, Fr Georges Florovsky, went to teach at Harvard and Holy Cross Seminary in 1955. He held this position until installing Fr Alexander Schmemann as dean in 1962. Archbishop Iakovos, former primate of the Greek Orthodox Archdiocese of America, which is now celebrating its seventy-fifth anniversary, made reference to Metropolitan Leonty as "a living saint.["]4

The essays that Metropolitan Leonty wrote at the beginning of the twentieth century in which he analyzes the unique character, conditions, and needs of Orthodox theological education in the North

---

4Metropolitan Leonty, a saintly and sage elder, wisely guided the Church during a remarkable period of stability, growth, and positive change until his repose on May 14, 1965, at the age of 89.

American context, may still be read with profit today. We will only recall, inspired by the presence of His All Holiness, two of the young rector's strongest convictions. First, he was convinced that the Church has always sought for her pastors "not simply the educated, but the highly educated," since "only education provides the versatility (*mnogostoronost*) which is indispensable for pastoral activity," enabling the priest to be truly "all things to all people"(1 Cor 9.22). Second, he insisted that there can be no preference in Orthodox theological education between the theoretical and the practical, or between the academic and the pastoral, especially here in North America.[5]

In honoring us with his presence, His All Holiness Patriarch Bartholomew does more than affirm the history and mission of St Vladimir's Orthodox Theological Seminary. He joins Metropolitan Theodosius, our president and alumnus, who this very day celebrates the twentieth anniversary of his election as our church's primate, and affirms with him, and the other bishops here gathered, the necessity for sound theological training, education, and scholarship in the Church. This is especially precious in this present time when there are some who say that academic theological study is unnecessary and even dangerous to the Church's faith, life, and mission in the world.

We who work in Orthodox theological education constantly affirm, and are ever ready to be reminded, that true Christian theology demands liturgical worship, personal prayer, ascetical striving, and pastoral engagement. We also constantly affirm, and rejoice to be reminded, that true Christian theology also demands diligent scholarly study, careful critical analysis, responsible intellectual reflection, unwavering respect for facts, and a relentless, courageous, and humble pursuit of truth wherever it may lead. For true theology and true scholarship, as His All Holiness himself tirelessly testifies, can never contradict the Lord Jesus Christ who is the Truth, nor betray or blaspheme the Holy Spirit who is the Spirit of Truth.

We admire Patriarch Bartholomew's efforts to lead us on the narrow path that leads to life in God. We honor his willingness to witness to apostolic Christianity, which, in St Paul's words, is always concerned with "whatever is true, whatever is honorable, whatever is just, whatever is pure, whatever is lovely, whatever is gracious, if there is any

[5]See Archpriest Leonid Turkevich's report on Orthodox theological education in America in the *Orthodox American Messenger*, the official journal of the *Russian-American Orthodox Mission*, 17.24, 1913 (in Russian).

excellence, if there is anything worthy of praise" (Phil 4.8). We see in the Patriarch's every speech and action the desire, using again the apostle's words, to "present [himself] to God as one approved, a workman who has no need to be ashamed, rightly dividing the word of truth," thereby teaching us how we "ought to behave in the household of God, which is the church of the living God, the pillar and bulwark of the truth" (1 Tim 3.15). For the "God and Savior" of the Orthodox Church truly "desires all people to be saved and to come to the knowledge of the truth" (1 Tim 2.3).

We heed the apostolic admonitions of our Ecumenical Patriarch. We strive, at his command and example, to reject every kind of religious nominalism that holds the forms of godliness but denies its power (2 Tim 3.5). And we also reject every kind of religious zeal which, to refer again to St Paul, is "not according to knowledge" (*kat' epignosin*), and so results in well-intentioned people who are "ignorant of the righteousness that comes from God" replacing God's righteousness with a righteousness of their own (Rom 10.1).

Many issues are debated in the Church today. They include issues of biblical exegesis and liturgical practices, ecclesiastical order and church organization, evangelical witness and ecumenical activity. They also include interpretations of dogmatic formulas, ecclesiastical canons, and historical events. We pray and thank God for an ecumenical patriarch who encourages the diligent study of the Scriptures, councils, canons, liturgical offices, patristic writings, and saintly witness, in pursuit of solutions to contemporary controversies that are pleasing to the Lord and beneficial to His people.

Many dichotomies and divisions are also appearing in our time that are alien to God's gospel in Christ Jesus and contrary to the teaching of the apostles and the testimony of the saints. These include supposed oppositions between the local churches and the Church as a whole, between the Church's ordained leaders and the fullness of the faithful, between hierarchy and conciliarity, authority and freedom, scholarship and asceticism, married life and monasticism. We pray and thank God again for an ecumenical patriarch who encourages us to meet together, as we are now doing, listening to one another, looking into each other's faces, outdoing one another in showing brotherly love, giving honor where honor is due, and bearing one another's burdens so as to fulfill the law of Christ.

In exercising his archiepiscopal and patriarchal ministry, His All Holiness Patriarch Bartholomew exercises the three dimensions of the episcopal office with his brother bishops. He shows himself as a *pastor* in imitation of the Church's one Good Shepherd. He shows himself as a *priest*, making present the Church's one High Priest. And, especially precious for us during his visit to St Vladimir's, he shows himself a *prophet* in obedience to the Church's unique and ultimate prophet, the Lord Jesus Christ himself, about whom the apostle Peter, invoking Moses, proclaimed: "The Lord will raise up for you a prophet. . . . You shall listen to him in whatever he tells you. And it shall be that every soul who does not listen to that prophet shall be destroyed from among the people" (Acts 3.22–23).

St Paul teaches that every member of the Church should desire the gift of prophecy. Surely theological educators must pray for this greatest of spiritual gifts. The apostle Paul tells us the purpose of the gift of prophecy. "He who prophecies," the apostle writes, "speaks to people for their edification and encouragement and consolation" (1 Cor 14.3). This is what we experience today in the visit of his All Holiness to St Vladimir's. We are edified, encouraged, and comforted to complete our course in fidelity to the Church's one Teacher who called us to share in his sufferings so that we might share also in his victory.

Knowing that "for a Christian," in the words of St Tikhon of Zadonsk, "authority and power are nothing but crosses," we offer our final expression of gratitude to His All Holiness Patriarch Bartholomew on this extraordinary day. We thank him for preaching the word of the Cross to us from the first moment of his patriarchal ministry, and for striving to live by the Cross in his daily labors. With "Christ and him crucified" as the content of his service, our Ecumenical Patriarch shows himself ready to preside in the love which God himself is, the God whose beloved Son was lifted up on the Cross in order to draw all people, with the whole of creation, to himself.

His All Holiness testified to the Cross of Christ and the love of God in his first address as ecumenical patriarch. He ended his message that day as I, in imitation of him, will end mine today. He repeated the words of the Church's first theologian, the simple words in which all theology is found and all ministry fulfilled: *O Theos agape estin*, "God is Love."

Theological Education
and Modernity[1]

The task of Orthodox theological education is basically two-fold: to affirm and explain the Orthodox Christian faith, and to assist believers in applying and practicing this faith in their daily lives. Likewise, Orthodox theological education has two basic require-ments. The first is "the knowledge of the truth" (1 Tim 2.4), for which we Orthodox regularly pray in our liturgical services. The second is the ability to "test the spirits" and to "discern the signs of the times" (1 Jn 4.1; Matt 16.3).

Knowledge and Discernment

We who work in theological education are engaged in a constant effort to discover the truth, particularly in regard to our specific educational tasks and pedagogical duties. As we struggle to pray and to be purified from our sinful passions, we continually study the Church's authorita-tive witnesses to Orthodox Christian faith and life: the holy Scriptures, the liturgical rites, the decrees of the universally received councils, the canons, the icons, the writings of the church fathers, and the lives and teachings of the saints. And we must continually increase our knowl-edge and develop our skills in the particular academic and pastoral dis-ciplines for which we are personally responsible.

We Orthodox theologians and educators also struggle for the ability to test the spirits and interpret the signs of the times. We must be aware of the realities of the world in which we live and work, acquiring eyes to see what is happening around us, ears to hear, and minds willing to understand. We must resist the temptation to flee into fantasy worlds of our own making. We must be delivered from all forms of delusion

[1]This talk was originally given at an international conference of Orthodox theological schools sponsored by SYNDESMOS in August 1994 at the Holy Trinity Monastery on the island of Halki in Turkey.

(plane, prelest). We must be engaged with our world without being enmeshed in it; and detached from our world without being contemptuous of its questions, indifferent to its desires, insensitive to its sufferings, and insensible to its need for salvation.

To accomplish the ascetical feat *(podvig)* of theological education is not merely difficult; it is humanly impossible. It becomes possible only with God who gives the grace of discernment *(diakrisis)* to those who struggle to know and love Him, and to know and love the people and places which He knows and loves. God works for good in all things with those who are called according to His purpose (Rom 8.28).

Faith in the gospel, knowledge of the truth, the gift of discernment, freedom from delusion, competence in one's scholarly and pedagogical discipline, and a dispassionate identification in love with everyone and everything for the sake of enlightenment and salvation are essential qualities for the ministry of theological education in the Orthodox Church. Our modern, post-Christian, post-communist (and, as some in the West now say, post-modern) world urgently demands these qualities from Orthodox pastors, theologians, and teachers.

Modernity and Post-Modernity

"Modernity" and "post-modernity" are understood differently by different people in different places. The terms which are used to describe our present human condition and approach to reality may also be understood differently by Orthodox educators in the same place, and even in the same country, church, and theological school.

I suggest that we do not attempt to define "modernity" or "post-modernity" in our present discussion; nor try to discover its origins, describe its characteristics, delineate its possible meanings, or enumerate the countless questions that it raises for Orthodoxy. I suggest rather that we reflect on five issues with which all of our Orthodox churches and schools must deal in the midst of "modernity" or "post-modernity," whatever our particular setting, and however we understand and use the terms.

Our five topics for discussion will be (1) permanency and change, (2) individuals and authority, (3) persons and communion, (4) unity and diversity, and (5) the communion of men and women. I will reflect briefly on each of these issues, and offer some personal thoughts to begin our conversation.

Permanency and Change

Radical change and relentless novelty in all areas of human life characterize our modern world. These challenge Orthodox Christians with a plethora of new and unprecedented issues, questions, and demands, as human persons and institutions experience the most rapid transformations and dramatic mutations in thought and behavior in human history.

Virtually all Orthodox churches and communities are experiencing a breakdown of the Church's living tradition while also experiencing an explosion of information about Orthodox theology, history, liturgy, and spiritual life. This ironic situation has produced a loss of balance and integrity in Orthodox thinking and activity. For example, some people know the Scriptures well, but know little about liturgy and the spiritual life. Some have read Bulgakov and Berdyaev, but have never read the Bible. Others are experts in the *Rudder*, or the *Typikon*, or the *Philokalia*, but have never had basic biblical teaching or catechetical instruction. Those with a basic education are among the learned few who immediately become teachers in church—with appointed or self-appointed positions. And this is occurring at exactly the moment when those within and outside Orthodoxy are demanding that Orthodox pastors and educators distinguish clearly between what is permanent and essential in Orthodox faith and life, and what is temporary and nonessential, and therefore changeable and dispensable in Christian belief and behavior.

When we look to the Bible and church history seeking insight about permanency and change in the Church, we see that the Church has a "human form" just as Christ does. The human form of the Church consists in all of its human expressions, such as Scripture, liturgy, and so forth, and has been constantly changing throughout the ages. The Church changes in history, Fr Alexander Schmemann used to say, in order to remain the same. The Church changes its forms of organizational structure, liturgical worship, doctrinal formulation, devotional practice, and relationship to secular powers in order to remain faithful to itself and its mission: to proclaim the gospel, confess the truth, and witness to God's love in the fallen, constantly changing world within which the Church exists as the gracious presence of God's kingdom.

When we look to the Bible and church history we also see that the Lord Jesus Christ, with his prophets and apostles, were killed for being innovators. Many of the church fathers and saints were also bearers of new things for the Church, and also suffered for their teachings. They brought new experiences of faith, new formulations of doctrine, and new forms of worship. This is true of the Cappadocian fathers, for example, and St. Gregory Palamas and his fellow hesychasts. In more recent times it was true of St Paissy Velichovsky and the Optina elders, St Tikhon the Confessor of Moscow, and St Silouan of Mt. Athos.

That the Lord Jesus Christ, the first Christians, and many Orthodox teachers and saints were accused of being innovators, and truly were so, does not mean that all who bring new things to God's people are holy and true. Many who have introduced errors and evils into the Church, and created heresies and schisms were also innovators. Their new things were not of God, but of the devil.

On the other hand, those who preserve old customs and teachings in the Church are not necessarily free from falsehood and sin. St Cyprian of Carthage said many centuries ago that antiquity is not truth (*antiquitas non est veritas*), and that ancient custom may be nothing more than ancient error. Many who are mistaken and create schisms and heresies in the Church may be "conservatives" who mindlessly repeat the good words of the Scriptures, councils, and saints while they distort the content of the teaching and fail to live by its truth. They thereby find themselves fighting against the truth when it comes in new forms in response to new questions and needs. The iconoclasts were such people, as were those who opposed the holy hesychasts.

The issue of what is changeable and unchangeable in Christian life and teaching has really nothing to do with antiquity or novelty as such. It is not about what is old-fashioned or modern, traditional or innovative, conservative or liberal. Christ has said, ". . . every scribe who is made a disciple for the kingdom of heaven is like a man who is a householder who brings forth from his treasure things *new* and old" (Mt 13.52). The issue of permanency and change is rather the more radical issue about what in the Church's life and teaching is right or wrong, true or false, edifying or destructive, of God or of the devil.

Much that is considered to be new in the Church is often not substantially new at all. It is rather a new articulation or expression of a truth that has always been known and believed. Sometimes what appears to be new is also nothing other than a rediscovery and recovery of something old that has been lost, forgotten, obscured or misunderstood.

Sometimes what is new is indeed truly new in the temporal and historical sense because it is something of God previously unknown that is seen for the first time. In such cases the reality itself is neither new nor old; it is simply newly known because its time has come.

Orthodox theologians and educators must make a careful and dispassionate study of the Bible and church history to learn how change occurs in the Church. We must come to see how Orthodox Christians remain faithful to Christ while receiving new knowledge, answering new questions, and formulating new expressions of doctrine and worship. We must learn how the Church throughout history has refashioned what needs refashioning while ridding itself of unacceptable teachings and practices that have crept into the Body. We must come to see how things that are merely temporal and temporary are permitted to pass away as peacefully and painlessly as possible. And, of course, we must learn to protect ourselves from new things that are not of God. Our times, perhaps more than ever, require that we make these efforts and acquire these gifts.

Individuals and Authority

How do Orthodox theologians and educators discern what is to be preserved or changed in the Church, welcomed or resisted? How do we answer new questions, meet new demands, and respond to new needs while remaining faithful to ancient and eternal truth? How do we protect ourselves against erroneous and evil innovations, while ridding ourselves of old deviations and distortions? How, in a word, do we determine what is right or wrong in Church and society, true or false, good or evil, acceptable or unacceptable, of God or of the devil? The modern world often tells us that our real problem is that we persist in raising such questions, thinking that they can be properly answered. It tells us that such questions and answers, especially in areas of religion, theology, spirituality and ethics are no longer objectively possible, necessary, or welcome. It tells us that there really is no right and wrong, true and false, good and evil in a metaphysical sense, surely nothing that we can know and prove, even if, for whatever reasons, we may still believe in God and spiritual reality.

In the modern view (with its roots in Cartesian and Kantian philosophy, Protestant theology and piety, and various Enlightenment versions of reality, particularly social and political) each human being is an "individual." Everything theological, spiritual, metaphysical and ethical is a matter of individual choice, subjective decision, and private belief. The only ethical boundary to an individual's belief and behavior is that it may not directly harm another individual, nor curtail his or her rights and freedoms in any way. (This is why, for example, in the modern debate about abortion it is critical to determine whether or not a fetus is an "individual.")

Even in churches and theological schools, individuals are free to pick and choose. They have the natural, some even say the "God-given," right to do so. They rely on a democratic state constitution to protect their liberty and sovereignty. They can think what they like and do what they want, taking from their "education" what they choose and leaving the rest. They have their private reasons for implementing their self-designed agendas, satisfying their self-determined desires, and fulfilling their self-identified needs—with the inviolable right to do so.

It is important to realize that all who accept the modern individualistic approach to reality are not necessarily "liberals." Some modern individualists are in fact quite "conservative," perhaps even reactionary. It just happens that "conservative" individualists have a taste for old things (like, for example among the Orthodox, medieval piety, or clerical styles of the Ottoman period, or non-revised calendars, or ancient languages, or outdated liturgical practices.)

While being totally "modernistic" in their attitude and spirit, which they would usually violently deny, conservative individualists curse things "modern" because they prefer things old. Even if they do not identify what they like from the past as eternal and divine, nor insist that all others follow it, they insist on their individual freedom and right to think and do as they please. And they insist as well, just like "liberal" modernists, that no "authority" in church or state has the right to tell them, or make them do, otherwise.

Individualists basically recognize no authority other than themselves. Not being anarchists, they usually admit the need for civil and ecclesiastical "authorities," but they seek those who agree with them and enforce their opinions and desires. When such people are religious, they follow the "god" of their choosing, whom they may even call the Father, Son, and Holy Spirit. When they go to church, even to an

Orthodox church—even as pastors, monastics, professors, or teachers—they go to the church (or jurisdiction) of their choice, based on their subjective opinion and desire of what the "true church" and "true Orthodoxy" are, and should be. They interpret the authoritative witnesses to the Church's faith and life through the lens of predetermined and prejudiced predilections.

A tragic condition occurs when those in authority have become infected—consciously or unconsciously—by the individualistic spirit. Still more tragic is when they deny that they are so poisoned: then their thoughts and desires become commingled and identified with the teachings and activities of the Church itself. In such instances these bishops, priests, teachers, and elders victimize their disciples with an "Orthodox" theology, liturgy, and piety of their own making. They may have great "zeal for God," as the apostle Paul once said of some others, "but it is not according to knowledge" and so they substitute for God's righteousness, a righteousness of their own (Cf. Rom 10.2–3).

The radical individualism that has blossomed in the modern world has produced a reaction that is also a characteristic of our times. This is the reactive and reactionary flight of many in our modern (or postmodern) world into romantic reconstructions of the past. Those making this flight often create or join cultic communities to fulfill their fantasies. They surrender their personal freedom and responsibility and blindly follow the commands of leaders, or appoint themselves leaders, who guarantee safe and secure protection against the evils of the modern world. Many who take this flight are burned-out refugees of radical individualism who have overdosed on individual choices, decisions, and actions. Some of them come to the Orthodox Church looking for such an escape from reality. And sometimes, alas, they tragically find what they are looking for, sometimes even creating it themselves.

Orthodox pastors, theologians, and educators must deal with the modern individualistic approach to reality, whether it is openly admitted or delusively denied, and the various reactions to it. Our first duty is to discern its presence among us and to free ourselves, by God's grace, from its insidious power. Then we must work to organize and administer our schools and carry out our educational ministries according to Christ and the Church as they really are, not according to our subjective interpretations or the imaginations of cultic leaders to whom we have sold our minds and surrendered our souls.

Orthodox educators must also care for those who have been gravely wounded by modern approaches to reality, both individualistic and reactionary. Our churches, schools, and monasteries are filled with spiritually, psychologically, emotionally, and even physically wounded people, some of whom need professional medical assistance and psychological counseling—which bring still more issues of "modernity" for us to evaluate and resolve. In dealing with the unavoidable therapeutic problems that have become part of educational work in Orthodox theological schools, we are compelled to begin with ourselves: we who lead and teach are hardly unscathed by the modern world and its varied effects, both of capitulation and reaction.

Persons and Communion

Those who teach and study in Orthodox theological schools today, together with the bishops, trustees, and administrators of our educational institutions, must discover the narrow path of exercising personal freedom according to Orthodox Christian faith within an ordered ecclesial communion of mutual respect, responsibility, and accountability. This "narrow way that leads to life" is generally incomprehensible to the modern (and post-modern) mind. A radical change of mind (*metanoia*) is needed for this saving way of traditional Orthodoxy to be found and followed, even by us Orthodox believers who have lost it through centuries of tragically complicated ecclesiastical, political, cultural, and spiritual processes.

We who serve in theological schools and institutions must be capable of teaching our students, by word and by deed, the way of personal freedom exercised in an ordered ecclesial communal setting. We must create the conditions where all may speak and be heard in a common search for God's truth by reference to the authoritative witnesses to Orthodox tradition: the Bible, liturgy, councils, canons, icons, fathers, and saints. Our theological students must learn how to "do theology" (as we now say in the West) not only by academic study combined with liturgical worship and spiritual striving. They must learn by observing how our schools, as well as our parishes, dioceses and local churches, are organized, governed, administered, and financed, and by participating in the actual life and operation of these ecclesial institutions.

There are basically two alternatives to the traditional Orthodox way of personal freedom in ordered communal and conciliar life in the Church. There is the way of authoritarian, dictatorial *tyranny* that occurs when ecclesial leadership is separated from authentic ecclesial communion and conciliarity. (Fr Alexander Schmemann labeled this sickness "ecclesiastical bolshevism.") And there is the way of chaotic *anarchy* that is inevitably produced when ecclesial conciliarity and communion, by design or neglect, are detached from authentically authoritative hierarchal order. In such instances the church, diocese, parish, or school degenerates into clusters of competing parties, interest groups, and even isolated individuals, each pushing for its own peculiar form of teaching and practice.

A strange combination of tyranny and anarchy results when church members, both leaders and disciples, fail to make common reference to the authoritative witnesses to Orthodox faith and life in an atmosphere of personal freedom, mutual trust, and common responsibility. This "tyrannical anarchy" or "anarchical tyranny" appears when leadership defends its authority against communion and conciliarity. Paranoid defensiveness demands unquestioning loyalty and obedience, while "democratic" forces under the guise of personal freedom and ecclesial communality defend individual choices and party interests. We in North America can testify to such an anomaly, and painfully we watch its approach in other parts of the world.

Unity and Diversity

A devastating aspect of the modern (and post-modern) world is the tendency to separate and isolate, to disintegrate and fracture. The spiritual and material are divided from each other, as are the metaphysical and existential, and the theoretical and practical. Faith and knowledge are opposed. Theology and piety are divorced. Freedom is put in opposition to authority as the individual person—or parish, province, tribe, or region—is placed against, rather than within, the larger community of family, church, society, nation, and world. Prophet is opposed to priest, charismatic to institutional, individual to corporate, private to public.

An essential task of Orthodox theological education is to expose this literally "diabolical" approach to reality, and to teach and demonstrate in action the proper relationship between unity and diversity in all areas of human life and activity. Orthodox theological schools and institutions, like the Church itself, must find the royal way of maintaining its essential unity with the diversity that true accord requires for its actualization in life.

Unity and diversity in a theological school that is truly Orthodox will exist between the academic and the pastoral dimensions of the educational program and process. It will exist between scholarly work and practical application, and between the educational process as a whole and the work of the separate pedagogical disciplines: Scripture, liturgy, history, patristics, dogmatics, languages, and the various courses of pastoral theology and practice. It will ensure the freedom for objective scholarship in proper relationship to the Church's received tradition, which is guided and guarded by the Church's episcopal authority in communion with the faithful believers. And it will also hold together the diverse elements essential to a full and complete program of Orthodox theological education: academic study, liturgical worship, spiritual formation, practical field experience, and community life and service.

Orthodox theological schools must be structured to ensure unity-in-diversity, and diversity-in-unity. Crucial to the structure is the mechanism for an obligatory ongoing communication among all those involved in the process: rectors, teachers, students, administrators, staff, trustees, and the bishops, priests, and laypeople of the Church. When such communication is not mandated by the institution's organizational and operational structure, the educational process will fail, as it will when any of the constituent bodies in the process are excluded from appropriate participation.

All involved in the life and work of a theological school must voluntarily accept its structure; but the structure must be carefully and purposefully implemented, with leeway for questions and revisions, along with clear procedures for its adoption, application, and amendment. All participants in the process must be willing to compromise and cooperate on practical issues for the sake of the common good and the ongoing effectiveness of the mission.

The Communion of Men and Women

Especially acute in Orthodox theological education today is the issue which many consider to be the modern world's most critical and crucial issue: the communion of men and women. This general theme includes countless questions about human being and life, human sexuality, marriage and celibacy, family life, the bearing and raising of children, and social, legal, and political behavior. It raises basic issues of biblical interpretation, church doctrine and practice, and personal, social, and medical ethics. It concerns the very nature and naming of God. It forces a radical examination of the relationship between Orthodox Christian tradition and the claims of modern philosophy, science, and human experience in a way which makes it a perfect "case study" for virtually every issue which the modern world presents to Christian Orthodoxy.

What we teach about the communion of men and women in our Orthodox churches and theological schools, and how we live out this teaching in our academic, pedagogical, sacramental, and spiritual activities may be the greatest single expression and example of our Orthodox engagement with the modern (and post-modern) world. It reveals what we think, say, and do about virtually all contemporary questions concerning divine and human being and life. And, it does so in response to the ways in which these questions are posed and answered, or not posed and not answered, in the situations in which we live and work.

In dealing with the issue of the communion of men and women in our churches and theological schools, we are dealing with the issue of permanency and change in its sharpest existential form. We are compelled to examine our teachings and practices about human sexuality in order to determine what in the Orthodox view is of permanent significance and value in human life. We are called to explain our convictions in ways that will inspire and enable contemporary men and women who are willing to understand and believe in Christ's gospel.

We will be successful in this task only when we learn to deal properly with issues of freedom and authority in the Church, and in Christian life generally; when we become capable of finding and fulfilling ourselves as persons within a hierarchal and conciliar communion in which the truth and love of the Holy Trinity are made accessible to our participation and imitation; and when we gain the ability to discover and affirm the unity among human beings, belief, and behavior together with the countless ways in which this unity is expressed and actualized by creatures through the gracious good-pleasure of God, in whose image and likeness all men and women are made. In fulfilling the task of Orthodox theological education as it concerns the communion of

women and men, subjective individualism and authoritarian domination must both be rejected. Those in authority must foster free and
open investigation and conversation on all issues in an atmosphere of
mutual trust and respect. Church leaders especially bishops, pastors,
and teachers must resist premature conclusions on disputed questions.
All of Christ's baptized and sealed members who participate in the
Eucharist must be permitted to speak and be heard on every question,
striving to make their case by reference to the authoritative witnesses
to Orthodox faith and life. And, all must be seeking "the mind of
Christ," desiring only to defend "the faith once and for all delivered to
the saints" (1 Cor 2.16, Jude 3).

Empowered by God's Grace

For Orthodox Christians responsible for theological education this
means that the Church must be rediscovered as Christ's living body
and bride, the "pillar and bulwark of the truth," the "fulness of him
who fills all in all" (Cf. 1 Cor 11, 1 Tim 3.15, Eph 1.21). The Church as
a living mystical and communal organism must become once again the
subject (and not the object) of theology and theological education, the
place within and from which (and not simply about which) theological
investigation, reflection, and education are conducted.

Orthodox theological education will occur in the Church, even in
the midst of "modernity" (and "post-modernity"), when we who are
responsible take up our task with humility and courage. It will occur
when we fully accept, with faith and love, the time and place where
God has put us. It will occur to the measure that we attain to mature
personhood, to the measure of the stature of the fulness of Christ, to
the glorious liberty of the children of God (Cf. Eph 4.13, Rom 8.21). It
will occur when we are freed from the complications and complexities
of this world—ancient, medieval, modern, or post-modern—which
"lies in evil," whose "prince" is the devil, and whose "fashion is passing away" (1 Jn 5.19, 12.31, 1 Cor 7.31).

Theological education will occur, ultimately, when our efforts are
guided, protected, and empowered by the grace of God, which always
and forever superabounds in the midst of abounding sin. *Ou de
epleonasen he hamartia hypereperisseusen he charis* (Rom 5.20).

On Teaching and Learning in an Orthodox Theological School[1]

Among the many controversies in the Orthodox Church today are disputes about theological education and theological schools. While most Orthodox would affirm the need for theological education, not all affirm the need for theological schools. Some question the necessity and even the propriety of residential graduate schools of Orthodox studies accredited by non-Orthodox and non-ecclesiastical agencies, with classes and credits, papers and exams, trustees and statutes, advancement offices and endowments. Those who affirm the legitimacy and need for such theological schools hardly agree upon their organization and operation, and their purposes and goals.

We Orthodox are not alone in our controversies about theological education and theological schools. Virtually all churches are engaged in such discussions. And virtually all seminaries, divinity schools, and departments of religion and theology in North American colleges and universities are pressed to define their purpose and mission—both to themselves and to those who question their reason for being. This goes on while teachers in these schools continue to clarify and explain their profession.

Testimony to this state of affairs is a collection of essays by fourteen of sixteen Roman Catholic and Protestant theology teachers who spent a week together for three successive summers in conversations about their calling. About two-thirds of the participants in these discussions were from seminaries and divinity schools. The others were from departments of theology or religion at colleges and universities. The papers from these meetings are published in a volume called *The Scope*

[1] Fr Thomas Hopko gave the Father Georges Florovsky Memorial Lecture at the annual meeting of the Orthodox Theological Society of America at Holy Cross Greek Orthodox School of Theology in Brookline, Mass., in June 2002.

of Our Art, with the subtitle *The Vocation of the Theological Teacher*.[2]
It is a book well worth reading.

My paper today, though stimulated by these engaging essays, is not
a response to them. It is rather a modest contribution to the conversation among Christian theology teachers about their calling and a summary of my convictions about teaching and learning in an Orthodox
theological school.

I was ordained a priest in 1963 after graduating from Fordham College and St Vladimir's Seminary. My teaching experience began when I
was asked in 1965 to give an undergraduate course in Eastern Christianity at Duquesne University in Pittsburgh while studying philosophy
there and serving as the pastor of a church in Ohio. In 1968 I became pastor of a small church in Wappingers Falls, New York, and began doctoral
studies in theology at Fordham while teaching at St Vladimir's. From
1978 to 1983 I lived near the seminary and taught there while serving as
a priest in a church in Queens. In 1983 I became a full-time professor
and chapel priest at the seminary. In 1992 I was elected to be the head
of the school, called in our terminology the seminary dean, and was
appointed rector of the seminary chapel. During this time I also taught
courses at Fordham, Columbia, and Drew Universities. I was the Ely V.
Lilly Visiting Professor of Religion at Berea College in Kentucky in the
fall of 1986. I also taught summer school at several colleges, including
the Buddhist Naropa Institute in Boulder, Colorado.

Some will surely take issue with my perspectives regarding theological education, but no one can question my experience in the field. My
experience, along with my love for theological education and my admi-
ration for those engaged in all aspects of the work—which include spiritual formation, pastoral care, counseling in various forms, and
institutional administration—qualify me, indeed compel me, to speak.

The Scope of Our Art

In the aforementioned volume, The *Scope of Our Art*, is an epigraph
from St Gregory of Nazianzus, whom we Orthodox call "the Theologian" and who is one of the patron saints of our Three Hierarchs Chapel
at St Vladimir's Seminary: "The scope of our art is to give wings to the
soul . . ." This poignant phrase is fully explicated in the original:

[2]L. Gregory Jones and Stephanie Paulsell, Eds., *The Scope of Our Art, The Vocation of
the Theological Teacher* (Grand Rapids, Mich.: Eerdmans, 2002).

> But the scope of our art is to provide the soul with wings, to rescue it from
> the world and to give it to God, and to watch over that which is in His
> image, if it abides; to take it by the hand, if it is in danger; or to rescue it,
> if ruined; to make Christ to dwell in the heart by the Spirit: and, in short,
> to deify, and bestow heavenly bliss upon, one who belongs to the heav-
> enly host.[3]

I am grateful to Fr John Behr, our seminary's patristics professor, for
helping me to see that St Gregory is speaking here about the healing of
body and soul. He begins with the art (*therapeia*) that on the one hand
(*te men*) protects the health and good habits of the flesh, and which, on
the other hand (*te de*), provides wings to the soul in the manner that he
so eloquently describes. His long sentence, typical as it is of Hellenis-
tic Christian rhetoric, is touchingly beautiful. It may even "give wings
to the soul" of the person who hears it. But, his words are only remotely
relevant to the vocation of teaching in a graduate school of theology in
North America today, even in an Orthodox seminary. Still less are they
related to teaching theology or religion in a contemporary American
college or university. They have, in fact, strictly speaking, little to do
with teaching theology at all.

The "art" (*therapeia*) about which St Gregory speaks in this passage,
and in his homily generally, is the prophetic, priestly, and pastoral ministry of a bishop (and, today, also a presbyter) in the Christian Church.
That the phrase should be used as an epigraph to a volume on "the
vocation of the theological teacher" in our present context is a handy
example of what, in my view, is at the heart of the matter in our present discussion.

The Heart of the Matter

The greatest problem today regarding theological education—as well as
the educational, pastoral, spiritual, and therapeutic ministries of the
Christian Church—is the mixing up and juxtaposing of unrelated realities. This mix-up occurs in purposes and goals of theological education; in the meaning and purpose of graduate theological schools and
departments of theology and religion; in what it means to teach and
learn in these institutions; and in the relationship of what goes on in
these schools.

[3]Homily 2.22, *On the defense of his flight to Pontus, NPNF*, Second Series, vol. 7, 209.

Symbolic of this confusion in theological teaching and learning (with all due respect for rhetoric) are titles of recent writings by Orthodox authors such as "Monasticism as True Marriage" and "Liturgical Singing as Icon" and "The Book as Icon" and "Icon as Scripture." This confusion also shows itself in *The Scope of Our Art* which contains essays called "Teaching as cultivating wisdom for a complex world" and "Teaching as a ministry of hope" and "Teaching as conversation" and "Teaching and learning as ceaseless prayer."

The crucial task in theological education today, and in church life generally, is to see things clearly, to name things precisely, to distinguish things properly, and to relate things rightly—to clarify and simplify, to avoid ambiguity and confusion. For Christians this means that theological education is the effort to see and explain things as they are in God. It is to show how all things hold together in Christ. It is the work of coming to see the truth of things, and thereby to be freed from ignorance and error. It is the task of seeing how truth is practiced, and thereby being saved from destruction and harm. In biblical terms, theological teaching and learning for Christians are about knowing and acting according to God as God is. They are about the God "who desires all persons to be saved and to come to knowledge of truth." (1 Tim 2.4) If this is so, it is critically important, today more than ever, that theological teaching and learning be carefully focused and soberly accomplished. It is obligatory that they be done with simplicity, clarity, precision and discipline.

For this reason I believe that in theological teaching and learning today, certainly in Orthodox schools, it is obligatory (to return to our example) to show that a book is a book, and an icon an icon, and singing is singing. It is to show that marriage is marriage and monasticism is monasticism. Insisting on such simplicity and directness in our teaching, in the most radical way, lessens the risk of mixing things up to the point where everything becomes anything that we want it to be and there is no longer a clear and distinct reality about which we are thinking and speaking.

Strictly speaking, theological teaching is neither "a ministry of hope" nor "a cultivating of wisdom for life in a complex world." Neither is it "conversation" or "ceaseless prayer," although these are all absolutely necessary and deeply interconnected. Neither is theological education a peculiar form of pastoral ministry, spiritual guidance, therapeutic counseling, social commentary, or political advocacy and action, although these also are necessarily related to theological teaching and learning. What follows is my assessment and explanation of what theological education is meant to be.

Schools, Teachers, and Students of Theology

To begin with, I am firmly convinced of the need for graduate schools of Orthodox theology in North America today: schools with their own self-determined and self-defined purposes and goals that operate strictly according to exactly the same standards as other graduate educational institutions. Such schools can assume their rightful place among schools of higher learning, to benefit from interaction and cooperation with them, and to take advantage of the resources and opportunities available to them all. This can be done without the least compromise to Orthodox Church doctrine and practice; indeed, it must be done for the benefit of the Orthodox schools as well as for others. And, it must also be done for the sake of the Orthodox Church's witness to what it believes to be true in the world generally, and particularly in the world of theological education.

Orthodox theological schools have only one purpose and goal: to provide theological education in an Orthodox Christian setting in which competent teachers teach competent students Orthodox Church doctrine, liturgy, history, and practice in a competent manner in order to come to knowledge of truth for the sake of its application in the real lives of real people in the real world in which they live.

This being said, an Orthodox theological school is first and foremost a *school*. It is not a church or a monastery. Neither is it a therapeutic center, spiritual commune, extended discussion group, organization for social and political commentary and action, or a place for propagating the *phronema* and *ethos* of one or another cultural tradition, however Christian or Orthodox that culture may claim to be.

In our North American setting such schools have to be graduate schools that enroll students with a sound education on a college or university level. Their sole purpose is to educate these students in the classical areas of Orthodox studies: Scripture, liturgy, history, theology, canon law, patristics, ethics, hagiology, church art and architecture, sacred music, and pastoral, pedagogical, homiletical, and liturgical practices. They ought also to provide language courses appropriate to such study, according to scholarly necessity and practical need.

The crucial requirement for students in such schools is their willingness and ability to study at this level within an Orthodox context. The sole requirement for teachers is their willingness and ability to teach their courses competently and fairly in the same Orthodox Christian setting, which they share with their colleagues and students on a daily basis.

While Orthodox tradition requires that pastoral ministries—especially those of bishops, priests, and spiritual elders—require age and experience, with some evident "shedding of blood," it is generally held that teaching can be done by committed persons who know their subjects well enough to teach them to their students in a clear and competent manner according to their educational level. Such teaching on any level will never be the mere conveying of information. It will rather be the ability to engage good-willed students where they are, and to inspire them—even in a sense to *compel them voluntarily* to work through the given subject of study for themselves, in dialogue with their teachers and fellow students, in order to understand, discuss, and strive to practice what they learn with freedom and authority.

A graduate theological school professor is first and foremost a teacher of those who will teach and care for others. He or she is not a research scholar, spiritual elder, psychological counselor, pastoral guide, or a priest or monastic. Neither is he or she necessarily a mystic, a saint, a sage, or a person possessing any peculiar charismatic qualities in addition to the gift of teaching. He or she is also not necessarily a teacher of the masses.

Theology teachers may be men and women with many gifts and talents, but they are teachers in a theological school for only one reason: they possess the ability to teach the teachable students in a formal educational manner and setting. This means that they know the content of their courses, surely beyond that of their students, and that they know how to teach those who are willing and able to learn. It means that they are able to read, think, speak, write, and listen, to conduct classes, to lead seminars, and to inspire and guide educational discussion and debate. It means also today that they are skilled in the use of information technology for teaching and learning.

Although a few graduate students of theology will go on to become teachers in graduate schools; the great majority will not. The majority of students come to Orthodox theological schools to learn to teach and serve people in various ministries within and outside the Church. They will be teaching and caring for the multitude of people who do not study theology formally. While teachers in theological schools may be able to teach on a popular level, this is not their specific task or calling. Their work is to teach those whose task and calling this is, especially those who are being educated to serve in the church's ordained ministries. Because of this, teachers in seminaries and divinity schools, certainly Orthodox schools, should themselves be graduates of such schools and be men and women whose Christian commitment is expressed in active participation in parishes and congregations. They cannot merely be academic professionals.

Those who teach theology and religion in universities and colleges should, in my opinion, also not merely be academic professionals. Nor need they be popular teachers. They should be spiritual, committed scholars who share their convictions with seeking students who deserve to have contact with the "real thing" in their studies, and not merely with studious people with no personal stake in what they present in their classes. A college course in Buddhism, for example, should be conducted by a practicing Buddhist scholar capable of teaching a variety of students in an engaged and engaging manner, with freedom and respect. It ought not be taught by someone outside the Buddhist tradition, however learned and sympathetic to Buddhism that person might be.

The gift and calling of theological teaching and learning is not for everyone. Indeed, it is for a few. Those without the vocation and talent for theological education cannot be successful in the task and should not be encouraged in it. Honesty and charity demand that these people be directed to other useful and blessed occupations.

Order and Integration in Teaching and Learning

There is an order of theology that must be strictly followed in all theological teaching and learning, especially that which goes on in a Christian theological seminary or divinity school. There is also a proper order and integration of the various fields of theological study that must be rigorously maintained.

The foundation of Christian theology is the biblical word of God. Knowledge of the Scriptures, especially the canonical writings of the New Testament, which for Christians interpret the older biblical writings, is foundational for all Christian teaching and learning. This traditional principle is often violated today, not only in theological schools but also in churches and monasteries. St Ignatius Brianchaninoff, a nineteenth-century Russian bishop, passionately insisted that "the commandments of the Gospel" are the sole foundation of monastic life (and of Christian life generally).[4] What the learned and holy bishop "offers" to his fellow monks and nuns about the obligatory order of ascetical and spiritual life can be easily applied to theological teaching and learning in Orthodox theological schools today.

Archbishop Anastasios of Albania (himself a professor of theology) made the same point in a recent visit to St Vladimir's Seminary. Too many members of the Orthodox Church, he lamented, particular those zealous for the traditions of the fathers, often remain uninformed by the writings of the fathers themselves. Unlike the saints, they begin with the upper stories of the building before examining the foundations. They discourse about lofty things without knowing the basics. They discuss, for example, God's supradivine superessence without a sound knowledge of God's gospel in Jesus. They go to the writings of Isaiah the Solitary and Mark the Ascetic without going first to Isaiah the Prophet and Mark the Evangelist. They are taken up with Berdiaev or Bulgakov without knowing the Bible. They are enthusiastic about the Jesus Prayer with little concern for either Jesus or prayer. Such disorder causes great confusion and harm in Christian life generally, and certainly in schools of theological study.

With the biblical Word as foundation and norm, Christian teachers and students of theology can engage the texts and rites of church worship, the writings and witness of church fathers and saints, the testimony of church councils and canons, and the message of church art and architecture in a fruitful way. They can apply what they learn to the practical issues of the contemporary church and world, which they also study and analyze within the light of the teachings first witnessed to in Scripture.

Christian theological schools structured accordingly prevent intellectual, spiritual, moral, and aesthetic chaos that makes theological

---

[4]He says this with passion in his book *The Arena: An offering to contemporary monasticism* (St Petersburg, 1867).

education literally impossible. They prevent a fraudulent dynamic that is dangerous and destructive to human and cosmic being and life.

Context and Discipline of Theological Teaching and Learning

The order and integration of theological teaching and learning in a seminary or divinity school demands a particular context and setting, with a particular spiritual and intellectual ascetical discipline.

Teachers and students in Christian theological schools possessing the gifts of their calling must be believers in the gospel who participate regularly in the Church's liturgical and sacramental life. They must be people under spiritual discipline, struggling to live by God's Word and Spirit in their daily lives. They must be people of ascetical striving and constant prayer. They must regularly confess their sins and seek spiritual guidance. They must be committed to keeping God's commandments. They must be people of moral integrity. When married, they must have the support of their spouses and, hopefully, their children. In a word, theological teachers and students in Christian schools must be struggling to be and do what every committed Christian is struggling to be and do. Their struggle, of course, is carried on in the specific ways that befit their vocation.

Theological schools today must provide liturgical, sacramental, pastoral, and psychological services for their faculties and students (and even their staff, when appropriate) with all due care and confidentiality. Those who teach and learn in our schools (together with our staff people) should be assured of such support as a normal part of their life and work. Those who lead our schools should see that their people get the guidance and support that they need.

Specific spiritual disciplines for Christian teachers and students of theology—surely those in Orthodox schools—may be stated in twelve simple principles that describe the expected character of people called to this vocation.

1 Christian theology teachers and students are men and women who grow and change in their knowledge of their particular subject and in their personal spiritual depth. The classical "eight vices" of the Christian ascetical tradition (gluttony, *porneia*, greed, anger, sadness, despondency [*akedia*], vanity, and pride) harm theology teachers and students in particular ways. They distort their intellectual vision,

darken their minds, confuse their thoughts, and prevent them from seeing, understanding, and explaining things as they are and doing things as one ought. Thus, theology teachers and students are to be involved in ceaseless study and debate, as well as ceaseless prayer and spiritual striving, with necessary assistance and guidance in order to be freed from the passions and vices that come from being in a corrupted world.

2 Christian theology teachers and students relate their particular subject of study (when it is not scriptural study) to the Bible as the foundational term of reference and norm. This means that the person of Jesus Christ as presented in canonical Scripture is the foundation and content of all Christian teaching and learning.

3 Christian theology teachers and students are learned in all subjects of their theological course of studies and are able to relate their particular subject to all other subjects in the program. For this reason, it is necessary that teachers in theological seminaries are graduates of such programs themselves.

4 Christian theology teachers and students are members of a team in a community of learning. This involves the disciplines of cooperation instead of competition, support instead of detraction, building up instead of tearing down, encouragement instead of ridicule, and relating instead of isolating.

5 Christian theology teachers and students work within a particular tradition and demonstrate consistency with that tradition. Given this basic intellectual and spiritual obligation, they also offer criticisms of their tradition—or certain new and different interpretations and understandings of it—when honesty constrains them to do so.

6 Christian theology teachers and students do not engage in *ad hominem* remarks or attacks but rather address the *content* of the issue in question. This principle applies whether they are critiquing the teachings of persons within their own or other traditions, orally or in writing, inside or outside of the classroom.

7 Christian theology teachers and students are duty-bound to offer reasonable, measured explanations when they disagree with a particular position or teaching.

8 Christian theology teachers and students work with the possibility that they, and their educational and ecclesial traditions, may be wrong and in need of correction and change.

9 Christian theology teachers and students receive criticism gladly, calmly, and patiently. When proven to be wrong, they accept correction with grace and gratitude, and humbly and courageously change their thinking and teaching.

10 Christian theology teachers and students never dismiss a position with which they disagree by invoking buzzwords or epithets. Labeling a teaching as "modernist" or "fundamentalist" or "superorthodox" or "ecumenical" (to note but a few of the more mentionable labels) adds nothing to the content of an argument. Well intentioned teachers and students stick strictly to the content of the question, pointing out what they see to be false and wrong, and stating clearly and kindly what they think to be right and true.

11 Christian theology teachers and students exclusively reserve the words *heresy, heretic,* and *heretical* for those who represent false teachings as being Orthodox, claim that their doctrine is that of the Orthodox Church, and subsequently divide the ecclesial community. They never apply these words to people who are simply mistaken in their teachings, whether within the Orthodox Church or outside its canonical boundaries. They also do not apply these words to non-Orthodox Christians who have inherited their Christian faith in ecclesial communities already long-separated from Orthodoxy, especially those making no claim to be members of the Orthodox Church or to be teaching its doctrine.

12 Christian theology teachers and students do not shame, embarrass, ridicule, scorn, or demean any person. Nor do they ridicule anyone's thinking and teaching. Their only weapons in the battle for truth are reasonable arguments supported by solid evidence made from clear consciences, with gentleness and respect for everyone and everything (Cf. 1 Peter 3.15).

The Holy Spirit in Theological Teaching and Learning

The grace of God and the gift of the Holy Spirit are essential in theological teaching and learning; it is radically wrong to oppose spiritual life to scholarly work. Still more false and destructive is it to vilify education as if it were something evil in itself, or, on the contrary, to claim that education can occur without reference to God's grace and the gift of God's Spirit.

God's grace and the gift of the Holy Spirit are necessary for every good work, including theological education in an academic setting. But they are not magical or mechanical powers that replace hard labor and human effort. On the contrary, they are exactly what enable and empower such necessary and blessed activities, and allow them to be faithfully and successfully accomplished.

In all teaching and learning, surely in that which occurs in an Orthodox school of theology, God's grace and the power of God's Spirit insure that the teacher and student are freed from passions that darken the intellect and distort human thinking and acting. They provide the power for people to be victorious over vices that inhibit, and even destroy, their ability to see things clearly, understand things rightly, state things precisely, and do things properly. There is no opposition between scholarly effort and gracious enlightenment, between human achievement and divine illumination. There is no opposition between loving God with all of one's *mind* and loving the same God (and all persons and things in and with God) with all one's heart and soul and strength.

Formal theological education is not everything and is not for everyone, but it is essential to the well being of everything and everyone. Without formal theological education on the highest level of competence, the human race and the Christian church cannot be what they are and must be in the modern world. And, without the gracious activity of the Spirit of Truth nothing can be what it is and must be, including, above all, teaching and learning in an Orthodox theological school.

On Preaching in Church[1]

The task of the preacher at a liturgical service of the Church is to deliver the message that God speaks through his risen Christ by the Holy Spirit's power to the specific gathering in that time and place. The homily at a Divine Liturgy, vespers, matins, baptism, ordination, marriage, unction service, funeral, or special service of prayer is spoken and heard only once. It is a unique word of God that has never been spoken or heard before and will never be spoken and heard again.

The liturgical sermon is normally delivered by the head of the gathered church community who is formally responsible for the preaching of God's Word. If it is not the bishop or presbyter himself who is preaching, the sermon must be delivered by someone whom he appoints and for whose words he is accountable to God and the people. Any baptized man or woman capable of preaching may, in principle, give the homily.

The liturgical sermon is preached from a "high place," from the ambo or pulpit. This shows without any doubt that what is being preached is the Word of God and not the opinion of human beings. The homily follows the reading of the Holy Scriptures and the proclamation of the gospel, which are also read from a "high place." The liturgical homily is not preached at another time or place during the service. Nor is it to be preached when the service is over. It is not mixed together with other words, such as announcements or personal remarks. It is not done while standing or walking about in a casual or conversational manner. It is not done from the floor of the nave, except when practical purposes may require it, for example because of acoustics.

Preaching God's Word is a sacramental act. It is an essential element in the liturgical action of God the Father, the Lord Jesus Christ, and the Holy Spirit. When the bishop or priest, or the faithful person whom he

---

[1]This abbreviated version of a more technical paper entitled "The Liturgical Sermon" was originally published in a special issue of *St Vladimir's Theological Quarterly*, Volume 41, Numbers 2–3, 1997.

appoints to the task, stands to deliver the liturgical sermon, it is truly
"time for the Lord to act" (Psalm 119.126).[2] There is no Christian
liturgy without the proclamation of God's Word. Believing Christians,
with catechumens and other good-willed persons, may have communion with God through his Word without participating in the Lord's
mystical supper, but they are not to partake of Christ's Body and Blood
in Holy Communion without first communing with God in his divine
Word: the way to the altar table is always by way of the ambo or pulpit. The condition for Holy Communion with the Lamb of God and the
Bread of Life is obedience to the Word of God, all of which are the Lord
Jesus Christ himself.

The liturgical sermon, therefore, is not missionary evangelizing, catechetical teaching, biblical exegesis, theological instruction, spiritual
direction, or pastoral counseling, though it must be connected to these
inspired tasks. It is also not a sharing of thoughts, opinions and experiences, or an offering of food for thought and discussion. It is most certainly not the preacher's time for baring his soul, sharing his troubles,
revealing his burdens, grinding his axes, or taking vengeance on his
enemies.

Preparing the Preacher

The bishop or priest (and everyone who may be called to preach in
church, in their own way) is always preparing the liturgical sermon by
his personal striving and his pastoral service to the members, and
potential members, of the church he heads, with whom he lives, whose
burdens he bears, and for whom he ceaselessly prays. To be effective in
his preaching, and in his spiritual efforts and pastoral service generally,
the homilist must "peruse the Scripture daily," as a church reader is
obliged to do at the service of his or her appointment to this ecclesial
office.[3] The words of a liturgical sermon emerge from the words that
the preacher speaks and hears at all times in his or her daily life and
work. These words come with grace and power only from the abun-
dance of a heart perpetually wounded, broken, purified, united,

---

[2]The Divine Liturgy in the Orthodox Church always begins with the first deacon saying these words from Psalm 119 to the officiating bishop or presbyter. They show that the
church's liturgy is a divine activity in which God works through his appointed servants.

[3]Some Orthodox bishops have formally appointed and tonsured women as liturgical
chanters and readers.

enlarged, inspired, and illumined by God's Word and Spirit through everyday service to the Lord.[4]

The necessary practices that prepare a person to speak true and meaningful words, and certainly the words of God in a liturgical homily, are prayer, fasting, acts of mercy to others, silence, and ascetical striving for virtue and holiness. The Scriptures and saints clearly witness that persons who do not pray and fast, who do not intentionally practice silence, both exterior and interior, and who do not strive to do merciful acts and to struggle in spiritual warfare with their passions and sins must never speak because they will have nothing godly and worthwhile to say. They must surely never speak the Word of God in a liturgical sermon.

The saints particularly stress the practice of silence as a condition for preaching and teaching, both at liturgical services in church as well as in other evangelical and catechetical settings. They do this not only because silence is an essential condition for knowing God and hearing his words that are to be delivered to others, but it is also a necessary condition for knowing the people with whom one speaks and to whom one preaches. St Ambrose, for example, dedicates the first chapter of his treatise on the priesthood to the necessity for those serving in the Church's pastoral offices to learn to be quiet. One who cannot be still, says the traditional teaching, will have nothing to say. His or her words will nothing but idle chatter and vain babbling.

The gifts which prayer, fasting, silence, acts of mercy, and ascetical efforts provide for the preacher are the dispassion, discernment, humility, and love that allow him to truly hear, listen, see, and perceive, and so to speak. Those who say true words, and surely those who preach God's Word, must know God, themselves, and others as they really are. This accomplishment, say the saints, is an achievement greater than raising the dead. It is rarely perfectly accomplished, but it must be ceaselessly sought and relentlessly pursued. It is God's greatest gift, given only to those who are themselves fully prepared to hear and do God's Word, to obey and follow what they see and hear from God. In a word, only those who are freed from the slavery of the vain imaginations of their own minds and hearts, and are liberated from their own versions of reality, can see and hear, and also therefore speak and preach

---

[4]See Matthew 12.33–37 and Psalms *passim*.

God's Word. The Lord "leads the humble in what is right, he teaches the humble his way" (Psalm 25.9).

Preparing the Preaching

Together with preparing to preach through the diligent study of the Bible accompanied by personal striving in prayer, fasting, silence, acts of mercy, and ascetical warfare with passions and sins, the preacher must prepare the sermon itself. This preparation always includes the following elements.

The first step is the knowledge of the specific liturgical occasion. Preachers begin their preparation by reflecting on all the elements of the given liturgical occasion and action. They carefully consider the specific conditions of the specific gathering to take place. It may the Lord's Day liturgy or a feast day service. It may be a baptism or marriage or funeral. It may be a liturgy at a special occasion, like a conference or retreat. The gathering may be one with a great variety of people. Or it may be mostly a particular group, like young people or seniors or students or sick people. A clear understanding of the uniqueness of the setting is crucial for a discovery of the unique Word that the preacher is to provide for the people who are present.

In making this careful assessment of the liturgical occasion, preachers must become thoroughly familiar with the words and rituals of the given service. They must especially study the Holy Scriptures being used: the Psalms and psalm verses, the readings from the Old Testament when applicable, and most particularly the Epistle and Gospel readings. The liturgical sermon, except in the most exceptional circumstances and for the most exceptional reasons, is always the explanation and application of God's Word given in the Scriptures to those who are gathered. Only in the rarest of cases should the homilist preach from and about something other than the biblical readings of the given liturgical service. When preachers do depart from this rule, they must take full responsibility before God for doing so, believing that the Lord, according to his divine will and inspiration, blesses this daring action.

In studying the biblical texts related to the service at hand, preachers study them in their original versions and languages, in accordance with the theological training they have received. Priests have been trained and ordained primarily for this purpose. If the preacher is a layperson assigned to preach by the bishop or priest, he or she must follow this same rule. Preachers need to have a basic and sound understanding of the Bible generally, and of the particular texts to be explained and applied to the people gathered.

There are many tools available to assist contemporary preachers in the process of preparing their sermons, such as interlinear Greek-English texts of the New Testament, annotated Bibles with variant readings and various translations, and concordances, lexicons, and commentaries of all sorts. Following the Church's fathers and saints, the preacher makes use of all the available tools for illumining and clarifying the texts to be proclaimed and expounded. If preachers fail to do so, they betray the task for which they were chosen, ordained, or assigned. They place themselves, and their hearers, in great jeopardy before God, who said through his prophet, "Cursed is he who does the work of the Lord with slackness or indolence" (Jer 48.10). Being warned and admonished by the words of the apostle who said that "those who teach will be judged with greater strictness" (Jas 3.1), the preacher will also have to answer to Christ who said that "on the day of judgment people will render account for every careless (or vain, empty, barren, or fruitless) word they utter; for by your words you will be justified, and by your words you will be condemned" (Mt 12.36–37). If this is so for our everyday words, how much more so is it for the words that are proclaimed in a liturgical sermon!

In addition to carefully considering the content and context of the specific liturgical occasion, with a detailed consideration of the biblical texts for the given service, liturgical homilists also must consider the specific character of the given gathering. They have to know their audience and meditate on their conditions, needs, and concerns. They must anticipate their difficulties, confusion, and questions. They need to explore what is currently occurring in their lives, what is going on in their communities, and what is happening in their worlds. Then, they have to ask God's help in seeing these things clearly and in relating to them accurately and appropriately in their preaching.

Especially at baptisms, weddings, funerals, ordinations, and other such special occasions, it is important for the preachers to be fully aware of the people involved in the events. They must know the persons being baptized or married or buried or ordained. They must know about their families. They must be familiar with their talents and limitations, their virtues and vices, their glories and their failures. They must learn everything that they can about them so that their words will be the unique Word of God that must be brought to bear as directly and concretely as possible to the actual realities of the occasion. Preachers commit the sin born of sloth and carelessness when they say things that are irrelevant and inapplicable to the people who are actually present and participating in the service. Above all, preachers must firmly resist the temptation of preaching to (or about) those who are absent.

In preparing the liturgical homily, preachers realize that they are not trying to decide what they would like to say. They are rather trying to determine what must be said in obedience to God's Word and the people who are present. Or, perhaps more accurately, the preacher comes to understand that his or her task is to hear what the Lord himself is saying and to find the words to deliver this divine Word in the sermon. In this sense, the liturgical homily is the act of objectively discovering and obediently delivering God's unique message. It is not the task of subjectively and arbitrarily producing and presenting one's own word.[5]

Words for the Word

According to the Scriptures, God's Word is always true, right, sure, pure, clean, just, and altogether perfect. It revives the soul, makes wise the simple, enlightens the eyes, and rejoices the heart. It is more to be desired than fine gold. It is sweeter than honey. It never changes. It endures forever (Ps 19.7–10). God's Word is living and active, sharper than any two-edged sword. It cuts to the division of soul and spirit, bones and marrow. It discerns the thoughts and intentions of the mind and heart. It lays bare and opens up all that is hidden and obscure and concealed (Heb 4.12–13).

The words of the liturgical sermon, being God's Word for the specific occasion, must also therefore be sure, right, true, sound, and just. They must ring with a brilliant simplicity, clarity, purity, and directness.

[5]I am familiar with a parish that took this "objective" character of the liturgical sermon seriously. For a time, participants of the weekly Bible study examined the Scripture readings for the upcoming Sunday and considered the liturgical setting, the life of the parish, the current events in church and society, and so forth. From this exercise, they discovered the close connection between their own convictions about what God was trying to say to them and the Sunday sermon.

They must be sharp and discerning, disclosing and revealing. Nothing should be in a sermon that need not be there. Nothing should be artificial, abstract, arbitrary, or superfluous. Nothing should be said or done merely for effect. Nothing should be there to satisfy the speaker, or, still less, to draw attention to the preacher. Nothing is to be said that is not for God's glory and the good of the people.

The good of the people varies greatly. God's Word for the people may sometimes be words of enlightenment and instruction. At other times they may be for consolation and comfort. On other occasions, they may be words of edification, exhortation, and encouragement. In other settings they may be words of guidance and direction. At other times they may be words of rebuke, correction, and even chastisement. They may also be words of warning and threat. They may even, on rare occasions, be questioning words, sentences intended to provoke or perplex or shake up an arrogant, haughty, indifferent, or self-satisfied people.

The Word of the Lord has many different forms, variations, and intentions. The preacher's goal in the liturgical homily is to express this Word in the right words in the right way with the right tone for the right purposes. This demands a struggle to find these words before standing to preach and stating these words as clearly as possible. Preachers should begin their sermon having as clear an idea as they can about what needs saying and how it should be said.

Classical terms of homiletics and rhetoric outline a program for correct preaching. Preachers first find the Word and decide upon the way it is to be delivered (*inventio*). They then arrange their sermon in a proper order (*dispositio*). They then seek the specific language and style, with fitting images and examples that the Word and the audience demand (*elocutio*). They then present the Word in their words, voices, bodily movements, and manners in the ways that the Word and their hearers require (*pronuntiatio*). Finally, they firmly grasp, mentally and spiritually, the unique Word for the specific setting (*memoria*). They must, to continue with traditional rhetorical instructions, discover and deliver the right *logos* for the given *ethos* with the proper *pathos*.

Preachers may use notes to help them to remember and to speak clearly and coherently. They may, if necessary, even read from a prepared text, though this is generally discouraged. And they must always leave room for the Holy Spirit to intervene and to inspire and direct their words in their actual process of preaching. In the end, preachers do well to heed Fr Alexander Elchaninoff's advice to work and pray to avoid giving the people the Lord's "bread of life" either raw and unbaked, or so overbaked and burned that the people receive "cold ashes" in place of God's living Word.[6]

When properly crafted in obedience to God's Word by the Holy Spirit's guidance, the liturgical sermon has an eloquence that comes not from homiletical talents and rhetorical skills, but, as the Troparion to St Gregory the Theologian puts it, by the preachers having sounded the deep things of God.[7] This divinely inspired eloquence inevitably includes some stuttering and stammering and lack of oratorical slickness: it must, because of the fearful majesty and awesome ineffability of the Word being spoken. Whatever the content and form of the message, when it is produced in this manner it will be a sacramental act of God's crucified and glorified Son Jesus Christ himself delivering the Word of his Father from heaven to those in his Church on earth (Heb 12.18–25). It will be God's Word to his people that is proclaimed, as St Paul says, "not in plausible words of wisdom, but in demonstration of the Spirit and of power, that your faith might not rest in the wisdom of men, but in the power of God" (1 Cor 2.4–5).

[6]*The Diary of a Russian Priest* (Crestwood, N.Y.: SVS Press, 1982) 220.

[7]Literally translated, this hymn in honor of St Gregory states: "The pastoral flute of your theology destroyed the trumpets of the rhetoricians, for you sounded the depths of the Spirit of God and you were thereby given the grace of eloquence." A freer rendering puts it this way: "The pastoral power of your theology vanquished the vanity of the orators, for you have sounded the depths of the Spirit of God and were granted the gift of eloquence as well" (cf. 1 Cor 2).

The Mission of the Orthodox Church in North America[1]

J esus Christ sends his Church into the world for the same purpose that God the Father sent him. The Church, with Jesus as its head, exists to manifest God as fully and completely as possible to humans, until Christ returns in glory to establish God's reign in the universe.

The Church's mission in North America today is gravely complicated and debilitated by massive confusion and disagreement about Jesus Christ: his person, his gospel, and his Church. For the Church's mission to be achieved, therefore, requires that certain convictions about Jesus be accepted and certain actions be accomplished.

Begin with Jesus

Everyone in the Church—first of all clergy and lay leaders—must be convinced that everything in the Church begins and ends with Jesus. This may seem all too obvious, but it must be emphasized since it is so easily forgotten and so often betrayed.

In many Orthodox Churches and church institutions, Christ and his gospel serve merely as a pretext for a variety of religious, ecclesiastical, social, and political ideas and activities that have little, if anything, to do with the Lord's mission in the world. These ideas and activities may be old-fashioned or modern, spiritualistic or secular, relativistic or sectarian, political or pietistic. They may be sophisticated or simplistic, intellectual or popular, refined or vulgar. But whatever or however they are, they are not rooted in Jesus Christ. Nor are they guided and guarded by the gospel image and teaching of and about Jesus and God the Father;

[1]This address was given at the Fourth International Conference of Orthodox Theological Schools held in Bucharest, Romania, in August 1996.

nor are they informed by the Holy Spirit who is always and everywhere the Spirit of God.

Since the Church's mission is Christ's own, it always begins with the person and doctrine of Jesus proclaimed in the synoptic gospels, the Church's basic proclamation (kerygma). Mission does not begin with theology (theologia), even the Church's first and original theology recorded in the Gospel according to St John. Nor does it begin with dogma or liturgy, spirituality or piety, mysticism or activism.

To be Orthodox Christians, men and women must first encounter Jesus in his humanity. They must hear his messianic words and see his messianic signs. They must come to confess him as "the Christ, the Son of the living God" (Mt 16.18). And, they must behold him crucified. Only then can they come to know and believe in him as the risen Lord. Only then can they confess and worship him as God's incarnate Word, one of the Holy Trinity; the one by, in, and for whom all things are made: the theanthropic Master and Head of the universe.

That Christian faith and life originates with the man Jesus is of supreme importance for Orthodox missionary activity. This rule applies as much for missionary work among the "cradle Orthodox" who have been raised in the Church from infancy as it does to adult men and women who enter the Orthodox Church from outside, whatever their background, knowledge, and experience. Before everything else, members of the Orthodox Church are "disciples of Christ" and "members of Christ" (1 Cor 6.15). They must, therefore, know Christ as he really is and accept him as such.

Christ and the Scriptures

To know Jesus Christ is to receive him as he appears in the Church's canonical gospels and as he is proclaimed and explained in the Church's canonized writings of the New Testament. Whatever actually happened historically (and who can really know?), the real Christ for the Orthodox Church is the Christ of the Gospels and Acts; the Christ of the writings attributed to the apostles John and Paul, and Peter and James and Jude. There is no other Christ for the Orthodox Church. A Christ produced by scholars, mystics, poets, or politicians—or even by creative theologians, charismatic elders, or crusading activists within or without the Church—is never the real and whole Christ of

Orthodox doctrine, liturgy, spirituality, and sanctity. He is surely not the Christ of Orthodox mission.

To know the real Christ requires a diligent and critical study of the Bible. Before anything else, Christians are disciples, that is, students (*mathetai*). They are students of Christ before they are his "members" as members of his Church. They are his disciples before they are his apostles and missionaries ("those who are sent"). And, they are certainly his disciples before they are bishops, presbyters, theologians, monastics, and elders of his Church.

Jesus appears in the Gospel narratives first as rabbi, master, and teacher (*didaskolos, magister*). He instructs his students in the right understanding of the Old Testament writings. Crucified in shame and risen in glory from the dead, he opens the minds of his disciples to understand the Scriptures. He explains to them how "the Law, the Psalms and the Prophets" speak about him (see Lk 24).

Critical study of Scriptures is a reading and hearing of the biblical words without prejudging or predetermining their meaning. Through such study, the student (who may in some circumstances be unable to read) wants to know what the writings actually say and mean, first for those who originally wrote and heard them, and then for people today, beginning with oneself. Such study uses all available means to illumine and explain (but not to constitute or determine) the biblical texts as written and received in the Church. It employs, for example, the knowledge of languages, literature, history, religion, geography, and archeology. It welcomes the guidance of those skilled in such fields. But though this study is done within the Church community with the help of others, it must also be done for oneself. Each individual believer must personally engage God's Word in the Bible. Without such engagement, especially today in North America, and especially by the Church's leaders, there is no genuine Orthodox Christian mission.

Bible and Liturgy

The hearing and reading of the Bible essential to Orthodox missionary work occurs in the context of the Church's self-actualization in corporate worship, that is, the church's liturgy. The Church assembled in Christ's name before the face of God in the Holy Spirit for instruction, petition, praise, remembrance, and thanksgiving is the hermeneutical condition and context for interpreting God's Word as recorded in the Scriptures. As such, it is the point from which the Church's apostolic mission originates and the point toward which its activity is directed.

Not only is the Bible read, heard, contemplated, and explained at Church services, but the services themselves also are thoroughly biblical in content, form, and spirit. Biblically informed believers have an immediate awareness and experience of the scriptural message in Orthodox liturgical worship. Or rather, more accurately, the God and Christ witnessed in the Bible become immediately accessible to believers in liturgical contemplation and communion in the Church.

Without a biblical foundation—what Fr Georges Florovsky[2] called "the scriptural mind" (whose loss he lamented)—Orthodox liturgy degenerates into just about anything but true Christian worship. It becomes in North America, for example, pathetic attempts to recreate romanticized versions of church services and devotion of other places and times. Or it becomes enforced enactments of ritual rules and regulation rigidly performed by rigorous defenders of "the right way of doing things" (whatever that "right way" might be). Or it becomes religio-cultural folk celebrations with all desired words, movements, melodies, colors, and sounds (often recorded on the latest audio-visual equipment) performed for the enjoyment and comfort of its participants and observers. But whatever it becomes, it is no longer the "reasonable worship" (*logiki latreia*) in the spirit and truth of Orthodox Christian liturgical worship.

For Orthodox mission to be real and true, those outside the Orthodox Church must enter liturgical and sacramental communion, and grow within it, by way of God's Word incarnate by the Holy Spirit "in words" in the Bible, and "in person" as Jesus of Nazareth. Only those already firmly established in this spiritual way can lead others into its divine reality.

Spirituality and Theology

Just as authentic Orthodox liturgy is rooted in Christ's gospel and guided by the Church's Scriptures, and, as such, serves as the

[2]Fr Georges Florovsky, dean of St Vladimir's Seminary from 1949 to 1955, was a leading Orthodox theologian of the twentieth century. Cf. Andrew Blane, ed. *Georges Florovsky: Russian Intellectual and Orthodox Churchman* (Crestwood, N.Y.: St Vladimir's Seminary Press, 1993).

hermeneutical setting for understanding the Bible, so too is Christian spirituality and morality. A separation of spiritual practice and ethical behavior from their biblical roots is one of the greatest dangers for Orthodox mission—and for Church life generally—in North America today. It is certainly not less dangerous than a separation of biblical studies from liturgical worship and spiritual striving.

Many men and women in North America are avidly interested in Orthodox spirituality. They consume Orthodox ascetical, mystical, and hagiographical literature. They practice forms of fasting, vigil, and prayer described in classical Orthodox writings. They make prostrations, venerate icons, visit monasteries, and seek out elders. They participate in Orthodox liturgical worship. When they are not members of the Orthodox Church, they often become members. Some even join monastic communities. But often, these people are not deeply instructed in biblical doctrine, and may not even be that interested in it. When this is the case, the result is not sane and sober Orthodox Christianity but a variety of superficial and unstable, if not plainly sectarian and idiosyncratic, "Orthodoxies."

The Orthodox Church's missionary activity is beneficial and fruitful for such men and women when the Church's apophatic, mystical theology and spirituality are firmly grounded in cataphatic biblical teaching. It succeeds when Orthodox believers—both those who preach and those who hear—are convinced that God's uncreated light and wisdom is Christ himself. It works when the Holy Spirit is always and everywhere identified with the Spirit of Christ who spoke by the prophets, established the priesthood, and inspired the Scriptures. It produces real Christians when transfiguration and deification are sought and found through co-crucifixion with Jesus in the mortification of sinful passions: taking up one's cross and keeping the commandments of God.

In genuine Orthodox Christian missionary activity, Tabor never replaces Golgotha as the center of Christian preaching and piety, just as Mark the Ascetic never supersedes Mark the Evangelist or Isaiah the Solitary—Isaiah the prophet. Missionary work is truly Orthodox when the sayings of Paul the Simple and John the Dwarf are sought and heard in submission to the saying of their teachers and guides, Paul, the apostle to the gentiles and John, the Lord's beloved disciple and theologian.

In order for Orthodox missionary activity to be genuine and true, especially in view of the widespread interest in Orthodox spirituality, great care and responsibility must be exercised in the Church's use of the fathers and saints. Patristic theology, with the writings of the fathers and saints, which is now so popular and fashionable (and marketable!), is often presented, consciously or unconsciously, in ways that cause it to be wrongly understood and used. Patristic theology becomes a kind of "thing-in-itself" detached from its biblical foundation, ecclesial setting, and historical context. It becomes for example, a theological or spiritual "school," or a metaphysical, mystical "worldview," disengaged from the Church and the gospel of Christ.

In such a misuse of patristic and hagiographic material, Jesus Christ may hardly be mentioned and becomes of little interest or importance. At other times the fathers are presented as mystical, perhaps even infallible, oracles that all allegedly say exactly the same things. What results is what Fr John Meyendorff[3] called a patristic "mythology," or a patristic "fundamentalism," radically contrary to what the fathers themselves, each in his own way, actually believed and taught.

Certainly, there is a "mind of the fathers," which the Orthodox Church identifies with the "mind of the Church," and even the "mind of Christ." It is the "scriptural mind" mentioned above. It is the attitude and approach to God and all reality in God, as revealed ultimately and definitively in Jesus Christ. To "follow the fathers" is to follow their path of obedience to God's gospel concerning Jesus. It is to do what they did, in the same spirit and way. It is not simply to repeat their words or to quote their writings with little knowledge, discrimination, or respect.

Preaching and teaching the deep and difficult doctrines that the church fathers forged in the heat of impassioned theological and spiritual controversy (often in the midst of great social, political, cultural, economic, and even military turmoil) requires extreme reverence and responsibility. It cannot be done quickly or easily. It cannot be done at all by those without training, guidance, engagement, and experience. This is a teaching of the fathers and saints themselves. When this rule is disregarded or violated, "missionaries" lead people into temptation rather than into God's kingdom; a catechumen may not become "twice as much a child of hell" (Mt 23.15) as his or her teacher, but surely he or she becomes twice as much a child of confusion and fantasy.

[3]Fr John Meyendorff was Professor of Church History and Patristics at St Vladimir's Seminary from 1959 to 1992, serving as dean from 1984 to 1992.

Slaves of All

Only those who have emptied themselves of everything their own and who live in unconditional obedience to God for the salvation of all can be apostles of Christ. Only those who identify totally with those to whom they are sent, taking their sins upon themselves and advocating for them before God without judgment can preach and prophesy in Jesus' name without self-condemnation. God only sends those willing and enabled by God's grace to suffer all things in love for Christ, the gospel, and those to whom the gospel is given.

The Orthodox Church's perfect example of apostleship is always St Paul. And, the perfect description of the Church's mission is forever to be found in St Paul's letters, especially those to the Corinthians, who in many ways resemble not only the neophytes in North American Orthodox churches today, but old-timers as well. St Paul defends his apostleship to the divided, factious, litigious, carnal, conjugally troubled, sexually confused, spiritually hedonistic, disorderly, and disbelieving Corinthians by recounting his sufferings. He presents his afflictions, persecutions, temptations and trials as proof that he is sent by the Lord Jesus. He boasts that he asks and takes nothing from anyone. He does not hide or deny his problems. He does not pretend to be what he is not. He flaunts his foolishness and weakness. He broadcasts his many graces. He numbers himself with the apostles who have "renounced underhanded ways" and "refuse to practice cunning or to tamper with God's Word, but by an open statement of the truth . . . commend (themselves) to every person's conscience in the sight of God" (2 Cor 4.2).

The apostle Paul is first among Christ's ambassadors who are "afflicted in every way, but not crushed; perplexed, but not driven to despair; persecuted, but not forsaken; struck down, but not destroyed . . ." (2 Cor 4.8–9). He describes real apostles as those whom people can consider only as the "servants of Christ and stewards of the mysteries of God . . . fools for Christ's sake . . . the refuse of the world, the offscouring of all things" who "bless when reviled, endure when persecuted, conciliate when slandered" (1 Cor 4.1, 9–13).

The apostle Paul, as all who are chosen and sent by God, claims to be totally free. He has no selfish interests or self-serving motivations in his mission. He wants nothing for himself except to be saved. And even

then, he wishes that he could be accursed and cut off from Christ for
the salvation of his brethren (Rom 9.3). He is God's slave, the slave of
Christ and the gospel, the slave of all to whom he has become all things
so that by all means he might serve for the salvation of some.

> Woe to me if I do not preach the gospel . . . for though I am free from all
> people, I have made myself a slave to all . . . to the Jews I became as a Jew
> . . . to those under the law I became as one under the law . . . to those out-
> side the law I became as one outside the law . . . to the weak I became
> weak . . . I have become all things to all people that I might by all means
> save some. I do it all for the gospel, that I may share in its blessings.
> (1 Cor 9.16, 19–23)

The missionary mind and method described in St Paul's letters is
largely absent from Orthodox Churches in North America today. For
the most part, church leaders and activists (clergy and laity alike)
appear singularly interested in gaining customers for their particular
brand of "Orthodoxy" who will then support their style of church life
and activity. We in North America rarely reach out to others for their
sake, on their terms, with sensitivity and sympathy for their ideas,
experiences, concerns, and needs, in order to win them to Christ and
the gospel. We more frequently seek them for our own sake, on our
terms, in order to get from them what we want for ourselves—which
may range from earthly power and prestige, to spiritual self-satisfaction
and consolation, to feckless followers for our particular cause or crusade, to warm, wealthy bodies to populate and maintain our church
institutions and properties. When we identify our wishes with the
Church's mission, and when we fail to see ourselves and our ideas,
actions, and desires in the light of the wholeness and fulness of Christ
and the Church, we fail as missionaries.

Begin with Oneself

Only those who are themselves being saved by faith in Christ through
God's grace are empowered by the Holy Spirit to serve as apostles. They
never cease working out their salvation in fear and trembling before
God who wills and works in them for his good pleasure: that all people
might be saved and come to the knowledge of the truth.

Those being saved by grace through Christ and the Holy Spirit take every thought captive for the sake of Christ and crucify their flesh with its passions and desires, lest they who preach to others themselves be disqualified. They beg God for the fruit of the Holy Spirit so that, having preached and prophesied and healed and restored—and perhaps even worked miracles in the name of Christ—they may not hear the awesome words of the Master on the Day of Judgment. "I never knew you, depart from me, you evildoers" (Mt 7.23). Filled with love and compassion, and pleading before God for their hearers, such missionaries and apostles use everything the Lord provides in order to share what they themselves have received. They cannot do otherwise, for the love of God compels them. They are God's slaves, and the slaves of all, in the perfect freedom found in Christ Jesus. Joyfully, gratefully, and eagerly they become all things to all people that by all means they may save some through their service.

We can be confident that God, who never leaves himself without witnesses, will find such people to carry on the mission of the Orthodox Church in North America today. We trust in the promises of Christ.

On Christian Mission,
Evangelism, and Philanthropy[1]

Real Christians of Spirit and Truth live in the abiding awareness that God exists and that God is Love. They consciously
acknowledge that they, with the whole of creation, are boundlessly loved by God in Christ. They confess that all human beings are
made in the image and likeness of God who is Love, for an unending
life that is found and fulfilled in loving as God loves. They witness to
God's love in this world in word and in deed. And, they do everything,
as the conditions of their lives allow, to express their convictions without bringing attention to themselves or scandalizing others.

Real Christians are also convinced that human beings have failed in
love from the very beginning. They believe, with the apostle Paul, that
man's primordial sin is the refusal to acknowledge God's power and
deity in the things that exist, with the refusal to give God glory and
gratitude for his boundless love in creation (Rom 1.18 ff). They corre-
late people's refusal to know and love God with thanksgiving and
praise with their refusal to love their fellow human beings and their fellow creatures. They know by experience that human sin starts with the
refusal to love God; this refusal then changes over time, with the help
of heredity and environment (nature and nurture), into an inability to
love anyone or anything other than oneself and one's own self-interested earthly projects and pleasures. This normal and habitual attitude
in human society is now valued as expressing the epitome of human
maturity, freedom, and strength.

Real Christians, therefore, view human sin as a generational and
communal phenomenon, a poisonous disease in the human family that
differs in its deleterious effects according to the various values, world-
views, and religions of families, tribes, and peoples. And so, they see sin

[1]Fr Hopko presented this paper at the Conference on Missions at St Vladimir's Seminary in February 2003.

not merely as a matter of egoistic individuals choosing wrongly on the personal level, but more as a corporate human tragedy, rooted in the lie that creatures can presume to decide upon and devise their desires independently of the God who is Love—who fashions them in love by his Word and Spirit for life according to his divine image in loving union with others.

Self-love (which is radically different from love for oneself as God's good creature) is therefore viewed by committed Christians as the fundamental human sin and the cause of all human injustice and misery. It is the rebellion (*apostasia*) against God that produces for human beings and their progeny a society and culture of darkness, destruction, and death.

Christians who know God as Love know also that there is no choice for human beings but to surrender to God and to love as he loves by his grace and power. Jesus proved this to them; he freely chose to live by God's love and to bring God's love, without condition or discrimination, to everyone and everything. In the language of Christian tradition, Christ had a free, natural human will, as all humans do, but he had no *gnomic* will for choosing.[2] Because he was perfectly free and always in communion with God his Father whose divine nature he shared while being perfectly human, Jesus, in a sense, never "chose" anything. He did not deliberate or decide. His will was always the will of his Father, as were his words and his works. This is witnessed in Holy Scripture in awesome sentences often quite difficult to render accurately in English. For example:

> Have this mind among you, which is yours in Christ Jesus, who, though he was in the form of God, did not count equality with God a thing to be grasped, but emptied himself, taking the form of a slave, becoming in the likeness of men, and being found in human form, he humbled himself becoming obedient unto death, even death on a cross. (Phil 2.5–8)

Or again:

> Although he was a Son, he learned obedience through what he suffered; and being (thereby) made perfect, he became the source of everlasting salvation to all who obey him . . . (Heb 5.8–9)

---

[2]St Maximus the Confessor was mutilated for this teaching, only to be vindicated by the Sixth Ecumenical Council.

And again:

> My teaching is not mine, but His who sent me. If any man's will is to do His will he will know whether the teaching is from God or whether I am teaching on my own authority. (Jn 7.16–17)

And still again, more simple and directly:

> As the Father has loved me, so have I loved you; abide in my love. If you keep my commandments, you will abide in my love, just as I have kept my Father's commandments and abide in his love. (Jn 15.9–10)

> A new commandment I give to you, that you love one another; even as I have loved you, that you also love one another. (Jn 13.34)

> If you know these things, blessed are you if you do them. (Jn 13.17)

Real Christians are convinced that since God exists and God is love and human beings are made in the image and likeness of Love, the only choice for human beings is to love. They accept God's love and love God in return by loving their neighbors, including their enemies, as their very selves. Scriptures attest to this obedience, servitude, and singular human choice: to return love to God, who creates, redeems, sanctifies, and glorifies (and we Orthodox always add *deifies*) all human beings and all of creation. Real Christians accept and return God's love by loving their neighbors, including their worst enemies, as their very selves.[3]

Christians hold this convicting truth as the source, content, and goal of their mission in the world, their sole reason for being, until Christ comes in glory. They identify themselves as a people called, chosen, commissioned, and empowered by the living presence of Christ and the Spirit in their lives, to bring the God who is Love to all peoples and things. Their mission is to love with God's love in every possible way. "As the Father has sent me, even so I send you," says Christ the Lord (Jn 20.21). Christians accomplish their mission of love primarily through works of evangelism and philanthropy.

---

[3]St Silouan the Athonite, after years of ascetical struggles during which the fires of hell constantly burned around him, came to know God's love in the crucified Christ and to know that "our brother is our life." Cf. Archimandrite Sophrony, *Saint Silouan the Athonite* (Crestwood, N.Y.: St Vladimir's Seminary Press, 1999) 371, *passim*. St Silouan follows the teachings of such fathers as Anthony the Great who said, "Our life and our death is with our neighbor. If we gain our brother, we have gained God, but if we scandalize our brother, we have sinned against Christ." Cf. Benedicta Ward, ed., *The Sayings of the Desert Fathers: The Alphabetical Collection* (London, 1975), Anthony, 9 and John the Dwarf, 39.

Evangelism and Philanthropy

God's will for human beings to love according to God's revelation of
love in his Beloved Son—the bonded slave obedient unto a shameful
death on the cross—creates and constitutes the Christian mission of
love in the world. This mission is accomplished in *words* by the proclamation of God's gospel in Christ to all people and nations. This Christian *evangelism* is always accompanied by teaching (*didaskalia*) and
confession (*homologia*) and defense (*apologia*) and witness (*martyria*).
And, it is accomplished in *works* of love for human beings performed
in concrete acts of mercy without condition or discrimination. This is
Christian *philanthropy* understood not merely as various forms of
charitable actions and almsgiving, but as sacrificial service (*diakonia*)
and witness (*martyria*) in all areas of human existence that contribute
to human dignity, freedom, justice, and peace on earth according to
God's gospel in Jesus.

God's Word in Human Words

However much we remind ourselves that what Christians *do* is incomparably more important than what Christians *say* (a truth constantly
repeated), evangelism still has to do, primarily and exclusively, with
words. *Speaking* is itself a significant form of *doing*, and true and right
speaking is itself rooted in true and right doing, for "he who does and
teaches [these commandments]," Jesus says in that order, "will be
called great in the kingdom of heaven" (Mt 5.19).

To evangelize, strictly speaking, is to announce God's gospel in Jesus
to all people, in words appropriate to them and their conditions. It is to
speak God's saving Word in human words that are perfect, sure, simple, right, pure, clean, true, and righteous altogether (Ps 19.7–9). Evangelism is to proclaim God's Word, finding the right words in the known
language that the hearers can comprehend according to the realties and
experiences of their actual lives. To evangelize in this way is not only
an act of love for humanity, an act of philanthropy; but also an act of
basic respect. It shows that we see those who are before us, that we
honor them and their situations and conditions, and that we care about
them and their lives in this world. It demonstrates that what we are
saying and doing is about *them*, not *us*; that it is for them; that it is

God's gift of his love for their well-being and joy, which we, however sinful and unworthy, are sent to deliver for their salvation, and thereby also for our own.

Evangelism and the philanthropy that accompanies it require our complete lack of personal and corporate self-interest. It demands our total detachment and disinterest. It requires that we identify fully with those to whom we are sent to speak and to serve. It demands that we have only their well-being in heart and mind. It demands that we rejoice in their salvation more than our own. It demands that we pray for them and advocate on their behalf before the face of God. It requires that we take their sins upon ourselves and identify with their failings. It means that we are ready to die with them and for them, if this be God's will. It means that we joyfully and gratefully affirm everything that is of God in their lives, while gently rebuking what is evil and false. It presupposes that we ourselves know the difference between what is of God and what is not, what is essential and what is accidental, what is truly important and what has no lasting value or purpose. It presupposes that we have the gift of discernment, ourselves knowing the difference between true and false, right and wrong, beautiful and ugly, healthy and sick, divine and demonic. Such discernment comes only to those whose own hearts are broken by God's merciful love. This grace belongs solely to those who know by their own "blood" God's great mercy on sinners, and who confess to be the first among sinners.

Words proclaimed as the Word of God but which are not really God's Word condemn the speaker and destroy the hearer. If we say, "Thus says the Lord" to people, it had better be the Lord who is speaking, and not us. If we say, "Hear God's good news" it had better be God's gospel that is heralded, and not something of our own making and imagination. If we interpret the Scriptures and make reference to saints, we had really better know what we are talking about. In the Gospels, Jesus, following all of God's prophets, speaks of this to the scribes and Pharisees. His words are recounted for his own disciples and are surely directed to those who call themselves Christians today.

> Woe to you, scribes and Pharisees, hypocrites! For you traverse sea and land to make a single proselyte (convert), and when he becomes a proselyte (convert), you make him twice as much a child of hell (*gehenna*) as you are yourselves. (Mt 23.15)

Not only must an evangelist's words be really the Word of God, they must also be words spoken with love for the good of the hearer. Words that are true but not spoken with love condemn their speaker, though by God's grace they may still enlighten and save those who hear them. The same is true for philanthropic acts of mercy done without love for people, but rather from pride, vanity, arrogance, judgment, or some other viciousness. Jesus' words from the Gospel affirm this:

> Not everyone who says to me "Lord, Lord" shall enter the kingdom of heaven, but he who does the will of my Father who is in heaven. On that day many will say to me, "Lord, Lord did we not prophesy in your name, and cast out demons in your name, and do many mighty works in your name?" *(And they perhaps also may say, "Did we not evangelize in your name, and practice philanthropy in your name, and hold conferences on missions in your name?")* And then will I declare to them, "I never knew you; depart from me you evildoers." (Mt 7.21)

We must also remember that true words of God spoken judgmentally push sinners deeper into sin, especially if they have not experienced love in their lives; so also do philanthropic deeds done with condescension and indignity. Awareness of intentions in speaking and acting, and awareness of the state of the receptive souls help to assure that words and deeds are holy, pure, and life-giving. Christ warns people, particularly his disciples, that they will give an account of their deeds and the spirit in which they have acted. He also warns that they will have to answer for all their words, not only wicked and false words, but useless, careless, barren, and vain words. Speakers in his Name also will account for their purpose in speaking and for the power (or lack of power) of their words to produce the fruit of God's Spirit in their hearers: love, joy, peace, patience, kindness, goodness, faithfulness, gentleness, and self-control (Gal 5.22):

> Either make the tree good, and its fruit good; or make the tree bad and its fruit bad; for the tree is known by its fruit. You brood of vipers! How can you speak good, when you are evil? For out of the abundance of the heart the mouth speaks. The good man out of his good treasure brings forth good, and the evil man out of his evil treasure brings forth evil. I tell you, on the Day of Judgment men will render an account for every careless (or barren, or vain, or empty) word they utter; for by your words you will be justified, and by your words you will be condemned. (Matt 13.33–37)

On Christian Mission, Evangelism, and Philanthropy 73

The same thing is true about philanthropic activities. Christian good works can only be performed in God's Name for the sake of his love and as signs of his love. They never demean or degrade those for whom they are done. They are never done asking anything in return, and they never have impure, hidden, or ulterior motives. Further, they never obligate others to join the Christian Church out of gratitude, fear, shame, embarrassment, or a sense of indebtedness. Hearers of Christian preaching and recipients of Christian philanthropy must remain free of any expectation to become Christians themselves and must retain their free and voluntary desire, consent, and commitment in making choices.

Our Contemporary World

In our contemporary world people hear many different words claiming to be God's Word and many different gospels claiming to be Christ's own. The demeanor and behavior of Christian evangelists also has severely harmed the credibility of God's gospel, even when God's Word has truly been proclaimed. Evangelists, particularly Orthodox Christians, are facing an antagonistic audience. Let me list but five points for Orthodox Christian evangelists to contemplate:

- Orthodox Christianity (whether with a big or little "o"), with little exception, is scorned and ridiculed, especially in the influential areas of information, education, and entertainment, particularly in Europe and North America.

- People devoid of a sense of sin—having no knowledge of godly love, seeing no value in or need for forgiveness, and possessing no fear of death (which they view as an "enemy" when they enjoy self-defined earthly pleasures and which they welcome as a friend when they no longer can do so)—consider the gospel to be "bad," not "good," news.

- Christian leaders, especially the clergy, are not honored in society. To be a priest, minister, missionary or monastic are no longer respected vocations, especially not for white males in the northern and western parts of the planet.

- With few exceptions, Orthodox Christians personally and Orthodox churches generally do not organize evangelical and philanthropic activities, despite the wealth of North American and European Orthodox Christians and the great needs—both spiritual and material—among millions of other people, including impoverished Orthodox Christians themselves. Moreover, good-hearted people who attempt such activities are often looked upon with disdain, suspicion, fear, and even anger by their brothers, sisters, and fathers in Christ.

• Christianity is becoming a thing of the past: North and South America, Europe, Asia, and Australia have experienced this shift. Christianity as a tribal, ethnic, or national religion is fast disappearing; if Orthodoxy remains within those familiar categories, it too is certainly doomed to vanish.

In his book *The Next Christendom, The Coming of Global Christianity*, Philip Jenkins gives the Orthodox Church only part of a paragraph in his work of nearly 250 pages, easily quoted in full:

> The Eastern Orthodox churches will suffer acutely from demographic changes, given that the church's numbers are so heavily concentrated in declining Europe. Presently, the Orthodox Church worldwide claims about 214 million followers, almost all in countries of eastern and southeastern Europe that are likely to be losing population steadily over the next fifty years. Although post-communist Russia has experienced a substantial Orthodox revival, demographic trends mean that the long-term future of the church must be in doubt. Falling birth rates will ultimately be more destructive to Orthodox fortunes than Muslim or communist persecutions ever were. Taking an optimistic population projection, Orthodox believers will by 2050 have shrunk to less than three per cent of the world's population, pathetically smaller than the early-twentieth century figure. In the worst-case scenario, the total number of Orthodox believers in the world by 2050 might actually be less than the Christian population of a single nation like Mexico or Brazil.[4]

I quote these few sentences about Orthodoxy from Jenkins' book not with demographic interests, but rather with concern for Orthodox missionary activity, both evangelistic and philanthropic, in our present and future world. I am worried about where Orthodox evangelists and

---

[4]Philip Jenkins, *The Next Christendom. The Coming of Global Christianity* (Oxford, 2002), 96. See also William Dalrymple, *From the Holy Mountain: A Journey among the Christians of the Middle East* (New York: Henry Holt & Company, Inc, 1999).

philanthropic workers will come from, who will support them, and what they will have to offer to those outside the Orthodox Church, including Christians and would-be Christians who are unhappy with the Christianity they have inherited or heard about. My concern is especially strong for North America, where the number of Orthodox Christians, many of whom are of a nominal, self-interested variety, is rapidly shrinking. We need only to consider that the entire registered membership of the Orthodox Church in America (OCA) is less than 35,000.

Jenkins's ominous words not only signify that Orthodoxy is virtually absent from "the next Christendom" that he describes and predicts, but they also declare the decline of traditional Christianity in these regions of the world, even among believers who are still formally connected to historical churches. Therefore, one wonders what will happen to the children of the fundamentalist, charismatic, ahistorical, tribal, and ethnic Christians whom Jenkins now sees forming the world's "next Christendom" in Latin America, Africa, and Asia. When we look to the old Christian churches of Asia Minor, Europe, the Middle East, Northern Africa, and North America, as Jenkins himself does, history and experience indicate that in a few generations these new Christian churches and movements will face the same menacing situation; especially if the United States continues to export its present and rapidly developing "way of life" to these regions. So then, what must we do and what can we expect?

Christian Action and Expectation

Orthodox Christians today can only do what real Christians have always done and expect what real Christians have always expected, demographers and their demographics notwithstanding. They can carry on their mission of divine love by preaching God's gospel and serving humanity and all of creation in Christ's name as their conditions and resources allow. In doing this, they can expect suffering and scorn from creatures, and peace and joy from God, with the promise of everlasting life. If this could happen, then one of the great mysteries of Divine Providence might be that the church that appears to have almost no place in "the next Christendom" predicted by Professor Jenkins—namely, the Orthodox Church—may prove to be the only church whose doctrine and worship are fully faithful to God's gospel in Jesus, despite the sins of its members and the insignificance of its size. As such, it may well be the only church that real Christians will be able to take seriously. The Lord can produce "garlands in place of ashes" as he has done before (Isaiah 61.3); for with God all things are possible.

For this miracle to happen, however, the Orthodox churches in all parts of the world, our "global village," have to die to their present Byzantine/Ottoman and imperial Russian structures and human institutional forms and live as Christ's one holy Church. In this death, they will not remain alone, but will bear much fruit, in a manner proper to God:

> "Truly, truly I say to you, unless a grain of wheat falls into the earth and dies, it remains alone; but if it dies, it bears much fruit. He who loves his life loses it, and he who hates his life in this world will keep it for everlasting life." (Jn 12.24–25)

The greatest obstacle to the evangelical and philanthropic mission of our Eastern Orthodox churches, and surely for our Orthodox ecclesiastical "jurisdictions" in America, is our unwillingness to deny ourselves and die to ourselves, humanly speaking, so that others may live through our loving self-sacrifices for their sake. This is why our churches, jurisdictions, dioceses, and parishes remain alone, bear so little fruit, and are filled with so much turmoil and trouble.

Self-interested Christian churches—concerned about the preservation of their institutional and cultural forms and expressions—cannot be authentically evangelical and philanthropic. Additionally, members of such churches often declare that they need not worry because they have Christ's promise that the Church (meaning *their* particular parish or diocese or patriarchate in its present historical form) will survive; they quote the Lord's words about "the gates of hell" being unable to "prevail against it (Mt 16.18)", and they cease to be real Christians. Likewise, their churches cease to be the one holy, catholic and apostolic Church of Christ.

Christ's one, holy, catholic and apostolic Church has no command from its Lord to be concerned for its earthly institutional survival. Rather, God directs the Church to lose itself for the sake of Christ and the gospel out of love for God and neighbor so that others may enter into the Body of Him who has been crucified, raised, and glorified.

"Abba, Father, all things are possible to Thee; remove this cup from me; yet not what I will, but what Thou wilt." (Mk 14.36)

When the hour had come . . . having loved his own who were in the world, he loved them to the end. (Jn 13.1)

"If any one comes to me and does not hate his own father and mother and wife and children and brothers and sisters (*and nationality and culture and ecclesiastical institutions*), yes, and even his own life, he cannot be my disciple." (Lk 14.25–26)

There is no Christian evangelical and philanthropic activity without suffering and death; just as there is no consolation without crucifixion, no glorification without humiliation, and no *theosis* without *kenosis*, in and with the crucified Christ. God's love, the only authentic love that eclipses all other loves, actualizes itself in our sinful world through this self-emptying, co-suffering path. It is therefore neither surprising nor accidental that the great Christian missionaries through the ages were always few and persecuted, a small band of saints fired with apostolic zeal who severely suffered even at the hands of their ecclesiastical leaders and fellow church members for the sake of those to whom they were sent.

So, we are back where we started, with our convictions about the God who is Love. May we join those who have proclaimed God's gospel in Christ and do good deeds in his name with the divine love that makes these actions God's own. And, may we work according to God's will for the world, which he boundlessly loves and for which he sent his beloved Son, the "apostle and high priest of our confession" (Heb 3.1).

"Except for these chains":
Evangelism, Dialogue, and Tolerance[1]

> And Agrippa said to Paul, ". . . you think to make me a
> Christian?"
> And Paul said, ". . . I would to God that not only you
> but also all who hear me this day might become such as
> I am—except for these chains." (Acts 26.28–29)

This final exchange between King Agrippa and St Paul recorded in
the book of Acts provides a perfect introduction—and conclusion—to our reflections on evangelism, dialogue, and tolerance.
The apostle Paul evangelizes Jews and Gentiles. He proclaims the
gospel in public and private. He preaches in synagogues, marketplaces,
and courts of law. He dialogues with governors, high priests, and kings.
He bears witness to Christ and makes apology for his convictions. And,
he is sent to Rome in chains. For two years he welcomes all who come
to him in great numbers desiring to hear his views. Again he evangelizes, dialogues, testifies, and defends; "preaching the kingdom of God
and teaching about the Lord Jesus Christ quite openly and unhindered"
(Acts 28). But tolerance of the apostle's activity does not last. The *Book
of Acts* does not record St Paul's execution. His death is recorded,
rather, in the hearts of those who honor, and perhaps even envy, his
chains and his blood.

Evangelism

The Greek word for gospel is *evangelion*. It literally means a happy,
blessed message. It is usually rendered in English as "glad tidings" or
"good news."

[1]Fr Hopko presented this paper at a Conference on Mission and Evangelism at Holy
Cross Greek Orthodox School of Theology in Brookline, Mass. in September 1993.

John the Forerunner, the Lord Jesus Christ, and all the apostles announced what the New Testament writings call the gospel of God. Or, the gospel of Jesus Christ, Son of God. Or, the gospel of the kingdom of God. Or, the gospel of the grace of God. Or, most simply and commonly, the gospel of Christ.

This good news is that God has spoken and acted fully, finally, and definitively in His Son Jesus Christ, God's incarnate Word. The blessed message is that by his crucifixion, resurrection, and glorification Jesus the Messiah has brought God's kingdom to the world. All evils are forgiven and repaired. All wounds are healed. Death is overcome. All nations and the entire creation are saved for unending communion with God through Christ and the Holy Spirit, who is the personal presence of God's kingship among believers until Christ the King returns in glory to establish God's reign in the universe.

Those who believe in the gospel die with Christ to this age and are sealed with God's Holy Spirit. They know God's coming kingdom as the Lord's very presence in their midst, in the face of which they continually repent, in function of which they continually work, and whose appearance in power they continually anticipate and petition.

Although some who believe in the gospel are called to be "evangelists" in the strict sense of the word, having the specific ministry to preach the good news, all who believe in the gospel evangelize by their very being. Their presence, with their words and deeds, are a heralding (kerygma) of God's words and deeds, a testimony (martyria) to God's truth and love, and an answer (apologia) for the hope that is in them, which is God's victory for all who accept salvation on the Day of the Lord.

Christian believers, and those called to evangelical ministry, are not concerned with results. They know that the fruit of their evangelism is in God's gracious hands. Their pure, joyful proclamation of God's wonderful work in Christ and the Holy Spirit heralds eternal life, divine peace and joy, and the gift of God's goodness, beauty, and truth, freely bestowed and freely received. They are, in this sense, disinterested in the number of converts produced; their concern is not conversion at all. Surely, they hope to "make disciples of all nations, baptizing them in the name of the Father and the Son and the Holy Spirit, teaching them to observe all things" that Christ has commanded (Mt 28). But they know, as the great missionary St Innocent of Alaska constantly affirmed, that no one comes to the Father except through Christ (Jn 14.6), and that no one comes to Christ unless they are given and drawn by the Father who sent him (Jn 6.44). The only task of genuine evangelists is to sow God's Word. Results are up to God.

Evangelists employ skills blessed and graced by God—knowledge, wisdom, discretion, insight, relevance, sensitivity, communication, and timing. They despise dissimulation, manipulation, gimmickry, and trickery. They do not force, coerce, terrify, or threaten their hearers. They do not view their efforts as a crusade, competition, or contest. They do not measure their success in numbers of converts. They expect no worldly advantages, including promises of divine assistance to make life go better in this fallen age.

Like the Lord whose gospel they preach, those who evangelize leave people free to accept or reject God's glad tidings. While they witness to the truth and defend their convictions, sometimes to the point of physical suffering and death, they never quarrel, argue, or fight. And, they certainly never judge, demean, or condemn those who reject them and their preaching. They rather say with Jesus, "If I have spoken wrongly, bear witness to the wrong; but if I have spoken rightly, why do you strike me?" (Jn 18.23). Again as with Jesus, evangelism is always ultimately accomplished in silence and fulfilled in death.

Our world is saturated with talk about Jesus, the Bible, and salvation— much of which is sacrilege and nonsense. Because the record of Christian witness is so poor (as Dietrich Bonhoeffer insisted), Christians must again win the right to speak. A strong case may be made that evangelists in our time must primarily be silent examples who demonstrate in action the "righteous, peace and joy in the Holy Spirit" with which St Paul identifies God's kingdom (Rom 14.17). In any case, words without the divine unction and power that comes through ascetic striving and the spiritual shedding of blood are not only ineffective and useless, however formally true they may be; but they are unto the condemnation and judgment of those who dare to pronounce them.

Dialogue

The New Testament testifies that there is no evangelism without dialogue. The Gospels present Jesus in conversation with all kinds of people. The *Acts of the Apostles* and the apostolic letters portray Peter,

Paul, and the other apostles in constant dialogue with Jews and Gentiles, as well as among themselves and with other Christians.

Dialogue has many purposes. It provides the opportunity for clarification and mutual correction. It allows for communion in truth and love, as well as for the discovery and disclosure of real disagreement and division. It gives the occasion for people to listen to each other in order to find a common mind for common action, or to realize that they hold incompatible convictions. Dialogue compels people to look into each other's faces, thereby preventing easy answers to difficult questions and simple solutions to complex problems. Dialogue precludes the caricature, calumny, and slander of an absent adversary. Dialogue prohibits the presentation of only one side of an issue and provides the possibility for God to act.

Christians engage in diverse dialogues, the most basic and essential of which is our dialogue with God, that is, prayer. Following the example of our Master, we not only speak in prayer, but also listen; not only ask, but also receive; not only question and inform, but also present ourselves to be informed and questioned by the Lord. Silent, attentive, receptive listening is an essential aspect of every dialogue beginning with prayer.

Christians and local churches communicate with each other within the greater Church, regionally and universally. Although communal dialogue enhances the well-being of the Church, its essential function is to allow the Church, by God's Holy Spirit, to discover and express the "mind of Christ" (1 Cor 2.10–16), to express the communion that is the Church's very being and life.

Conciliar dialogue in God's presence with prayer, attention, and silence belongs to the Church's nature, being, life, and mission. Without it, there is no ecclesial communion and no evangelical activity. There is, the saints tell us, only deceit and delusion (in Greek, *plane*; in Slavonic, *prelest*).

Christians and local churches are obliged to dialogue with each other, especially when they have basic disagreements. They must meet, speak, listen, and pray until they find unity in God, even when there seems to be no hope of resolution and communion. This is especially so when each claims to have the "mind of Christ." Refusal to dialogue, particularly with those claiming to be Christian, gives victory to the devil, as noted in Scripture:

... let us consider how to stir up one another to love and good works, not neglecting to meet together, as is the habit of some, but encouraging one another, and all the more as you see the Day drawing near. (Heb 10.24–25)

Christians are to welcome, with gratitude and hope, dialogue both within the Church and among separated Christians and churches that work to clarify misunderstandings, remove disagreements, overcome divisions, deepen communion, recover unity, and foster cooperation and common activity. Irresponsible, careless, cynical, or self-serving participants must not betray fruitful dialogue. Likewise, Christians must not oppose or reject such dialogue, but rather engage in it with respect and good faith. They must strive for authentic and real, and not merely verbal and formal, conclusions and results. Common statements without common understanding, commitment, and action are, once again, not only empty and vain, but they also condemn and judge those who make them.

Likewise, when teaching those who have not heard the gospel, or have heard it wrongly, or in a distorted form, Scripture requires evangelists to respond to questions and objections "with love"—putting away bitterness, wrath, anger, clamor, slander, and all malice (Eph 4.15, 31). Christians are to make their *apologia* with "gentleness and reverence." They are told to keep their "conscience clear so that when [they] are abused, those who revile [their] good behavior in Christ may be put to shame (1 Pt 3.15–16).

We have many meetings today, on all subjects, in all situations, both within and without the Church. But do we have authentic dialogue that images the divine dialogue between God the Father and the Son in the Holy Spirit? Do we have a speaking and hearing, at least from our side, which is honest, humble, hopeful, and true? Do we have dialogues in which God can act?

Tolerance

Effective evangelism requires not only dialogue but also tolerance, the willingness and ability to endure the presence and practices of disagreeing and disagreeable others with patience and peace. Christians want tolerance in societies where they are minorities, since they are neither dangerous nor subversive to the common good. They view themselves

as a positive presence, even for those who disagree with their convictions. They have always defended their right to exist in situations
where they have been outlawed, persecuted, imprisoned, and killed.

Christians, in turn, therefore, are obliged to tolerate non-Christians
and non-Orthodox and even unbelievers in their midst, opposing them
only when their activities are overtly evil. They must not seek or support the Church's political and legal establishment, since history has
clearly proven this to be detrimental to evangelism and contrary to dialogue. Inevitably, this leads to theological error, ecclesiological confusion, government control of church activity, and spiritual malaise
among the people for which we Orthodox and other Christians are pay-
ing dearly.

Tolerance means that we coexist peacefully with people whose ideas
and manners differ from our own, even when to do so is to risk the
impression that truth is relative and all customs and mores are equally
acceptable (as happens in North America.) Tolerance never means that
we remain idle before wicked actions that harm human beings and
destroy God's creation.

Tolerant people are neither indifferent nor relativistic; they neither
sanction injustice nor permit evil, since injustice is intolerable and evil
has no rights. The only weapons that Christians may use against injustice and evil are personal persuasion and political legislation, both of
which are to be enacted in an atmosphere of freedom and respect. While
Christians are permitted under certain conditions to participate in
police and military actions to enforce civil laws and to oppose criminal
activities, they may not obey evil laws nor resort to evil actions for any
reason, certainly not in the alleged defense of good. This means that
Christians are inevitably called to suffer in this age, and perhaps even
to die. This is our gospel, our confession, our witness, and our defense.

Together with St Paul, Orthodox Christians truly want all people to
become "such as we are." And, like the apostle, they are compelled to
add, "except for these chains." For "these chains," invisible and spiritual though they may be, which are often placed upon us not with
spears but with sneers (as Dostoevsky has said), are essential to our
gospel. We can never practice evangelism, dialogue, or tolerance without them. They accompany our faith in the Crucified Lord.

The Orthodox Parish in North America[1]

T he word *parish*, like the word *diocese*, originally denoted a geographic territory. A parish was a region of a diocese. The head of an Orthodox church in a parish was the parish priest (presbyter). The head of the diocese was the bishop who served as pastor of the diocese's main parish church.

The words *parish* and *diocese*, at least in North America, no longer signify geographic territories or regions. Today an Orthodox "parish" is a community of Orthodox Christians served by one or more priests, perhaps with one or more deacons and other various ecclesial functionaries. An Orthodox "diocese" is an association of such communities headed by a bishop, who may have auxiliary bishops helping him administer his "diocesan" collection of "parishes."

This situation has never existed in Orthodox history until its appearance in early twentieth-century North America. Now it exists not only in the United States and Canada but also in other areas of the so-called "Orthodox diaspora," such as South America, Western Europe, and Australia. It has also recently appeared in places formerly having territorial Orthodox dioceses and parishes, such as Ukraine, Russia, and Estonia.

Voluntary Associations

Orthodox parishes and dioceses in North America today are, sociologically speaking, voluntary associations of like-minded Orthodox

[1]This keynote address was given at a conference on *The Orthodox Parish in America: Faithfulness to the Past and Responsibility for the Future* at Holy Cross Greek Orthodox School of Theology in Brookline, Mass., in September 2001. It was also used in a revised form as a study paper for the 13th All American Council of the Orthodox Church in America in Orlando, Florida in July 2002.

Christians, organized for purposes determined by their members. An Orthodox parish, and even a diocese, can exist for any number of reasons: spiritual, national, cultural, ideological, political, or even personal. A parish belongs to the diocese of its choice, most often on its own terms. This is ultimately true even when a parish originally was founded through a diocesan, rather than simply a parochial, initiative. In some cases parishes do not belong to any diocese at all; or belong only nominally to insure a minimal measure of ecclesial legitimacy. When members of an Orthodox parish in the United States or Canada experience a dispute that leads to a division into one or more "parishes," the resulting "parishes" usually end up in different "dioceses."

There are countless reasons why such a situation now exists in North America, all of which demonstrate the loss of Orthodox Christian consciousness, understanding, and behavior. Our present task is not to deal with the reasons for the present situation; it is rather to state the essential things to be believed, understood, and done if Orthodox parishes in America are in full accord with traditional Orthodox teaching and practice.

One, Holy, Catholic, and Apostolic

An Orthodox parish, that is, a local community of Orthodox Christians with one or more priests, has only one God-given reason for being. It exists to be the one, holy, catholic, and apostolic Church of Christ. Whatever the original reasons and conditions for its founding, whatever other services and activities it may provide, whatever other desires and needs it may fulfill for its members, the parish must be Christ's one holy Church. If it is not, then it is neither Christian nor Orthodox, whatever else it may be and do.

A parish must be *the* Church of Christ, and not simply *a* church, because, according to the Orthodox faith, every local community actually is the one Church of Christ. Theologically speaking, there are not many Orthodox Churches; there is only one. Each parish, therefore, must be the one and only Church of Christ.

The parish must be holy because Christ's Church is holy; because it is from God, about God, and for God. All parts of a parish are to be sanctified by the holiness of God and his Son Jesus Christ, "the holy one of God." All aspects of a parish are to be inspired and empowered by God's

Holy Spirit, who is the Spirit of God and of Christ. Nothing in the parish, therefore, is "merely human" or "secular." Everything in and about a parish—its organization, structure, administration, finances, and properties, as well as its theological and moral teachings and practices and its liturgical and sacramental rites and services—must be determined by God, inspired by God, and submitted to God for his glory and the good of his people. Everything in the parish must be "*theanthropic,*"[2] so to speak, if the parish is to be Christ's holy Church.

The Orthodox Christian parish must also be catholic. That a parish is "catholic" means it is full, complete, and whole; lacking nothing in its mystical and sacramental being and life. The word *catholic* literally means "full" or "whole" or "complete"; it does not, in the first instance, mean "universal" or "worldwide." In an Orthodox Christian parish the whole fullness of God must dwell, as in Christ's Body, with all the fullness of life and grace and truth, by the indwelling of the Holy Spirit.

Thus every local Christian community, every "parish," theologically, mystically, and sacramentally, is to be "Christ's Body, the fullness of him who fills all in all" (Eph 1.23). It is to be "the household of God, which is the church of the living God, the pillar and bulwark of the truth" (1 Tim 3.15). Everything in the parish is to participate in God's fullness and wholeness. Everything is to express it. Everything is to testify to it. Whatever is merely human, partial, fragmentary, and incomplete has no place in an Orthodox parish. Whatever, in a word (and playing on words) is merely "parochial" is not to be there. Obviously a parish will be particular and limited in empirical, cultural, and sociological forms; it has to be, since it is made up of human beings. But all of a parish's particular aspects, with all of its teachings, services, and activities, if they are Orthodox and Christian, will be open to the boundless fullness of God and will thereby be inclusive of everyone and everything that is good and holy and true, to the measure that this is possible given the actual people who comprise the community.

Finally, according to the Nicene Creed, the Orthodox parish must be apostolic, in at least two meanings of the term.

First, it is apostolic because it is founded upon Christ's apostles and is firmly rooted in apostolic doctrine and tradition. Not only should it keep and live "the faith which was once and for all delivered to the saints" (Jude 3), but it also should preserve and pass on the apostolic

---

[2]*Theanthropic* means equally divine and human.

"deposit" (*paratheke*) that has been guarded and developed, particularly through church hierarchs from apostolic times to the present (1 Tim 6.20; 2 Tim 1.12, 14).

Second, an Orthodox parish is apostolic also because it continues God's mission, which is the mission of Jesus Christ, the Holy Spirit, and the apostles of all ages. The Greek word *apostelo*, from which the words "apostle" and "apostolic" are derived, means "to send," as does the Latin word *mitto*, from which are derived the words "mission" and "missionary." According to the Scriptures, Jesus the Messiah is himself "the apostle" (Heb 3.1). According to his scriptural testimony, especially in the Gospel according to St John, Jesus speaks the words, does the work, and accomplishes the will "of the Father (or the one) who sent" him (cf. Jn 6.29, 44; 7.28, 33; 17.3.18). Likewise, the apostles, being filled with the Holy Spirit, are sent into the world by Jesus to proclaim the gospel of God's kingdom. "As the Father has sent me, even so I send you. . . . Receive the Holy Spirit" (Jn 20.21).

An Orthodox Christian parish, however it was founded and for whatever purpose is was organized, must understand itself to be an apostolic community with a missionary purpose. Its members, especially its leaders, must be conscious of themselves as people sent by Christ from God and empowered by the Holy Spirit to bring God's unity, holiness, and fullness to all human beings in this divided, sinful, and fragmented world. If a parish has no awareness and consciousness of being "sent" by God to speak his words, to do his work, and to accomplish his will in this world, then it is not an Orthodox Christian parish. At best, it is a bunch of decent people carrying on a bundle of benign activities for their own benefit. At worst, to use apocalyptic words, it is a "synagogue of Satan" perverting God's gospel by its "blasphemy against the Holy Spirit (which) will not be forgiven, either in this age or in the age to come" (Rev 2.9,3.9; Mt 12.31–32; Mk 3.28).

Prophetic, Priestly, and Pastoral People

For an Orthodox parish to be Christ's one, holy, catholic, and apostolic Church, its members must understand themselves to be a prophetic, priestly, and pastoral people. By faith and grace, they are called to actualize the presence and power of Christ—God's unique messianic prophet, priest, and pastor. They are to view their overseer as the ordained prophet, priest, and pastor who ensures that "God is with us" through Christ his Son; they are to constitute "a chosen race, a royal priesthood, a holy nation, God's own people" by the Holy Spirit (1 Pet 2.9).

As a prophetic, priestly, and pastoral people, the members of an Orthodox parish are to keep God's commandments as their essential and exclusive reason for being. Jesus describes the goal of the life and activity of an Orthodox Christian parish, made by Christ to be a prophetic "kingdom, priests to his God and Father" (Rev 1.6):

> And one of the scribes . . . asked him, "Which commandment is first of all?" Jesus answered, "The first is, 'Hear, O Israel: The Lord our God, the Lord is one; and you shall love the Lord your God with all your heart, and with all your soul, and with all your mind, and with all your strength.' The second is this, 'You shall love your neighbor as yourself.' There is no other commandment greater than these." (Mk 12.28–31)

In the Gospel according to St Matthew, Jesus teaches, "on these two commandments (Deut 6.5 and Lev 19.18) depend all the law and the prophets" (Mt 22.40). For our present purposes, we can also say that on these two commandments depend the whole being and life of an Orthodox Christian parish as a community of prophetic, priestly, and pastoral people.

Heart: Liturgical Worship and Sacramental Service

Jesus says that God must be loved first of all with all one's heart. In biblical usage, the heart is the center of a person's being. It is the ground of a person's life, the seat of a person's will, and the source of a person's activity, beginning with one's words. It is the "place where God bears witness to himself," according to St Isaac of Syria; the place in a person, according to St Macarius of Egypt, which contains God himself, and Christ and the Holy Spirit, and the whole of creation, visible and invisible, spiritual and material, good and evil. A person's heart reveals what he or she really is, and really thinks, and really wants, and really does. "For where your treasure is," Jesus tells us, "there will your heart be also" (Mt 6.21).

The heart of a parish, if it is Christ's one holy Church, will be totally given to God. In this sense, the heart of an Orthodox Christian parish will be its liturgical and sacramental worship. Worship will constitute the parish's core. It will be the parish's essential mode of self-realization. It will be its basic reason for being, the foundational purpose for its existence and life—otherwise, it will cease to be an Orthodox Church.

An Orthodox Christian parish exists to praise, bless, and glorify God; to ceaselessly sing the Thrice-Holy Hymn to the life-creating Trinity. It's essential purpose is to baptize people in the name of the Father and the Son and the Holy Spirit; to enable them to die in Christ and to be raised with him to newness of life; to be sealed with the gift of the Holy Spirit; to hear God's Word, to respond to God's gospel, to participate in the eucharistic sacrifice of Christ's Body and Blood; and to actualize God's kingdom on earth, in spirit and truth, by faith and grace, until Christ comes in glory at the close of the age.

If an Orthodox parish is not fundamentally liturgical and sacramental, if it is merely an association which provides cultic rites to its members, often for a fee, as they desire and demand, then it is not an Orthodox Christian church. It is, as we have said, at best a center of benign and benevolent activities, some of them "religious" and some of them "secular," enacted by order of its members; and at worst, it is a "synagogue of Satan," which will not be forgiven its blasphemy against the Holy Spirit.

Soul: Spiritual Life and Pastoral Care

An Orthodox Christian parish must also be a community of people loving God with all their souls, as God's law commands and Jesus confirms. The word *soul* (Greek *psyche*, Hebrew *nefesh*) literally means *life* and is often rendered as such in contemporary English translations.

Loving God with all one's soul means loving him with all of one's thoughts, words, and deeds in the routine thinking, talking, and working of everyday living. For an Orthodox Christian parish, if it is Christ's holy church, this means that the community as a whole, and each individual member of it, is personally committed to living a Christian spiritual life by struggling to keep God's commandments. "If you love me," Jesus says, "you will keep my commandments. And I will pray the Father, and he will give you another Comforter (Greek: *parakletos*: counselor, advocate) to be with you forever, even the Spirit of truth, whom the world cannot receive, because it neither sees him nor knows him; you know him, for he dwells with you, and will be in you" (Jn 14.15–17).

Christian spiritual life affects every aspect of a person's being and every area of a person's life and work. It influences body and behavior, as well as thoughts and feelings. It determines private and personal activity as well as public and political action. But people need help in living a Christian spiritual life in its fullness and depth. People's rationally-animated bodies do not mechanically become "members of Christ" and "temples of the Holy Spirit" (1 Cor 6.15–19). A person's enfleshed spirit does not magically possess the "mind of Christ" (1 Cor 2.16) and become "one spirit" with the Lord (1 Cor 6.17).

Members of Christ's Church must have spiritual guidance and direction. They require pastoral attention and care. They need instruction in "fighting the good fight" by learning how to resist temptation, to reject evil thoughts, and to overcome sinful passions by partaking, through faith and grace, in Christ's victory through the Holy Spirit. Such spiritual and pastoral services must be present in an Orthodox Christian parish if it is truly Christ's holy Church. Although they need not, and indeed cannot, be provided by the clergy alone, bishops and priests, however, are duty-bound to see that these services are provided by people capable of doing so, for the benefit of those willing to receive them. The Orthodox Christian parish is the proper place for this to happen. If it is not happening, then, once again, the parish community is not Christ's Church.

Mind: Education and Enlightenment

Members of an Orthodox parish, if they are to be Christ's holy Church, must totally mobilize their efforts to love God with all of their mind, through enlightenment and education. Jesus' first title in the Scripture is *rabbi*, which means "teacher" or "master" (Greek: *didaskolos*, Latin: *magister*). As messianic pastor and priest Christ is also "the prophet" who brings ultimate and lasting judgment upon those who hear and reject him (Jn 1.21,6.14; Acts 3.22–26). The Lord's first followers are called disciples, or students. And the first thing said about those who believed in God's gospel of Christ crucified and glorified is that they "continued steadfastly in the apostles' doctrine" (Acts 2.42).

An Orthodox Christian parish, therefore, is essentially a teaching and learning community. It is a school of disciples whose master is Christ as he speaks within the company of believers, especially through the pastors and those with the charism and training for teaching and preaching.

An Orthodox parish without well-prepared evangelical and exegetical sermons at its liturgical services, and well-prepared doctrinal and catechetical sessions as part of its educational ministry, whatever else it might have, including having lots of liturgical services and loads of social events, can hardly be an Orthodox Christian church The inclusion of educational ministry is crucial to the parish appearing as a Christian witness to the community without, especially in the face of scorn and ridicule by society; and it is crucial to the parish being a source of spiritual nourishment to the community within, especially since members now join parishes because of choice and conviction, instead of convention and custom.

Strength: Mission and Philanthropy

Loving God with all one's strength, particularly according to the Hebrew text of Holy Scripture, means that we are to love God with all that we possess, primarily our money and property. Strength, in this context, does not merely mean mental, emotional, or physical might, though these, of course, are not to be excluded from our love for the Lord.

An Orthodox Christian parish, when it is Christ's holy Church, is obliged to use all of its powers for God's glory and the people's good. Christians as individual persons, as well as families, parishes, and dioceses, will have to give account to Christ for how they used their God-given strength. We will have to answer for our use of money and resources, property and possessions, positions and profits. We will be asked how we loved "in deed and in truth," and not merely "in word or speech," through concrete acts of charity for the hungry and thirsty, the sick and suffering, the homeless and naked, the persecuted and imprisoned (cf. 1 Jn 3.18; Mt 25.31–46).

On judgment day, the Lord will not ask us about our parish size and facilities. Nor will He be interested in our liturgical schedule or style. He will not ask us how we dressed or what we ate. He will be indifferent to how large our church temples were, or where they were located, or how they were decorated and appointed. Nor will He ask us to recite the Nicene Creed, or to explain the doctrine of the Holy Trinity. All of these things are essential, but their significance has only one end: the love of God with all one's heart, soul, mind, and strength, expressed, as it can only be expressed in this present age, in concrete acts of love for our neighbors; first of all the members of our own families and churches, and most all for those who hate and oppose us.

Love of God with all our strength through acts of love for our neighbors and enemies is enacted primarily through evangelism and philanthropy. Sacramental participation in an Orthodox parish is strictly reserved for committed Orthodox Christians who take full responsibility for the Church's faith and life and completely identify with the Church's path through history; but the philanthropic and evangelical activities of an Orthodox Christian parish, as well as its services of teaching, counseling, and prayerful intercession, have no bounds or limitations. They are to be exercised freely and without discrimination for all people regardless of their religion, nationality, race, sexual behavior, or relation to Christ's Church. The first Christians, as witnessed in the New Testament writings, and such saints as John Chrysostom and Olympia, and Fr John of Cronstadt and Mother Maria Skobtsova, taught and practiced this Christian truth without the slightest hesitation, equivocation, or compromise.

A parish without carefully planned and implemented evangelical and philanthropic activity directed both within and outside its parochial bounds, is, once again, simply not Orthodox or Christian. This is especially the case when huge sums of money are collected in parishes through secular activities, and spent primarily, if not exclusively, for self-serving parochial purposes, like the salaries of the parish employees (including the clergy), or the acquisition of unnecessary properties and luxurious liturgical appointments.

Structure and Administration

The parish requires a proper Christian structure and administration in order to provide proper worship, education, pastoral care, spiritual direction, evangelism, and philanthropy. The head of the parish in its total life must be the chief parish presbyter who is ordained and assigned by the diocesan bishop. This does not mean that the parish

priest functions merely as the bishop's "representative" or "delegate."
It means rather that he is appointed by the bishop and accepted by the
parish as the community's spiritual and sacramental leader, father, and
pastor. He is the head of the Body who images and presents God and
Christ in every aspect of the Lord's messianic ministry.

The Christian parish headed by its priest shows that it is truly
Christ's holy Church, and not merely a human association of like-
minded people incorporated to satisfy the demands and desires of its
members. When properly functioning and structured, the parish main-
tains its identity and integrity as Christ's Body, the household of God.
It realizes itself in a sacramentally ordered hierarchal and conciliar
structure. In this way, as Fr Alexander Schmemann[3] used to say, a secularized hierarchy opposed to conciliarity is prevented from exercising
tyranny, and a secularized community opposed to hierarchal leadership
is protected from succumbing to anarchy.

The parish priest, properly understood in Christian Orthodoxy, is
neither a domineering despot nor a servile hireling. He is neither an
authoritarian "stand-in" for an almost always absent hierarch, nor a
lackey at the beck and call of a parish board. He is rather a called,
trained, tested, and ordained teacher, pastor, and priest who guarantees
the presence and action of Christ in the community. His God-given
task, confirmed by the pleroma of the faithful, is to beget children to
God through God's Word and Spirit, and to empower every parishioner
to find and fulfill his or her calling as a member of Christ's Body. He is
the servant of God's servants, for God's glory and the good of all people,
including those outside the parish community, whoever they may be.

Unity and Variety

Until God's kingdom comes with power at the end of the age, Orthodox Christian parishes around the world will be struggling to be
Christ's holy Church. These parishes, certainly in the United States
and Canada, will be of a great variety of sizes, shapes, and styles, though
each one, theologically and mystically, will be the very same Church
of Christ. The parishes will be composed of different kinds of people.

[3]Protopresbyter Alexander Schmemann, Dean of St Vladimir's Orthodox Theological
Seminary from 1962 to 1983 and a leading Orthodox theologian, died in 1983 at the age
of 62.

They will be of different cultures and traditions. They will have different emphases and possibilities in worship, education, pastoral care, and philanthropic and evangelical activity. None of them will claim that they can do everything by themselves. All of them will admit that they need each other, being constrained by truth and love, to cooperate for God's glory and the good of God's people. They will all confess that to do God's work they cannot compete with each other, but must complete each other in Christian service and ministry. They will know that the only way in which they should strive to outdo each other is in expressing godly zeal, brotherly affection, honor, and mutual respect (cf. Rom 12.9–13).

The priests in these God-guided parishes will pastor their people not by lording it over them, but by giving their life to them in godly service with diligence, patience, and love. They will not look for the kind of parishes they want, with parishioners prepared to satisfy their ideological, liturgical, and pietistic passions. They will rather humbly and gratefully serve the actual parishes they are in, identifying by God's grace with the people whom God has given them. The guiding rule for such priests will be forever provided by the apostle Paul who became "all things to all people, that (he) might by all means save some" (1 Cor 9.22).

Whatever confusions and difficulties confront Orthodox Christianity in North America today, whatever their origins and causes, and whatever temptations and trials they bring to believers, there is no good reason why an Orthodox Christian parish in the United States or Canada cannot be Christ's holy Church. All that is required is that its members, beginning with its leaders, be firmly resolved to have it so. Their afflictions will be great, as Christ has promised, but their successes are assured by his victory. "In the world you have tribulation," Jesus says to his apostles, "but take courage, I have overcome the world" (Jn 16.33). "For what is impossible with men is possible with God" (Lk 18.27).

The Work of Christian Laity[1]

n St John's Gospel the people ask Jesus the question, "What must we do, to be doing the works of God?" Jesus answers them, "This is the work of God, that you believe in him whom God has sent" (Jn 6.28–29). In the same Gospel the Lord also says these startling words: "Truly, truly I say to you, he who believes in me will also do the works that I do; and greater works than these will he do, because I go to the Father" (Jn 14.12).

These two teachings—that to do the work of God is to believe in him and that those who believe in him do the very works that he does, and even greater works because he has gone to the Father and has sent the Holy Spirit—are repeated in many different ways in Holy Scripture. The apostle Paul affirms these teachings in his well-known words that are often only half quoted:

> For by grace you have been saved through faith; and this is not your own doing, it is the gift of God—not because of works, lest any man should boast. For we are his workmanship, created in Christ Jesus for good works which God prepared beforehand, that we should walk in them. (Eph 2.8–10)

Christian Scripture teaches us, often from the mouth of Jesus himself, that believers in God and in Christ are to hear the Word of God the Father, and to keep it. They are to do God's work. They are to accomplish God's will (cf. Mt 12.50, Mk 3.35, Lk 8.21,11.28). They are to perform the good deeds that prove and complete their faith, for as the apostolic doctrine ascribed to the Lord's brother James insists, "faith by itself, if it has no works, is dead" (cf. Jas 2.14–26).

---

[1]This paper represents an abbreviated combination of several retreat talks entitled "The Work of God's People," given both at St Vladimir's Seminary and at a meeting sponsored by Orthodox Christian Laity in Cleveland, Ohio, in October 2003. The original retreat talks are available on cassette and CD recordings from SVS Press.

The good works that Christians are to accomplish through their faith in God, and by his working in them, are connected to their love for God. The first and greatest commandment for Christians is to love God with all their mind, heart, soul, and strength. All that Christians think, want, do, and have is to be wholly devoted to loving God, through Jesus and the Holy Spirit.

According the teachings of Christ and his apostles, Christians can actualize their love for God only by loving their neighbors, including their worst enemies, as their very selves. Believers in God are to love one another with the very love with which God in Christ loves them. This is Christ's "new commandment" to his disciples, to "love one another, even as I have loved you" (Jn 13.34,15.15).

Good works inspired by faith in God and in Christ are always accomplished by the Holy Spirit "through whom God's love has been poured into our hearts" (Rom 5.5). God's works are always works of love. They are acts inspired and accomplished by God's mercy. Those who act without love, St Paul teaches, even when their works are objectively "good works," and even when they are marvelous and miraculous, are "nothing" and "profit nothing" (cf. 1 Cor 13.1–3). This is because good works, including miracles, can be done without love. They can be performed from pride, vanity, malice, envy, and judgment of others. When this happens, these works are done unto condemnation. Christ himself testified to this terrifying truth in his Sermon on the Mount:

> Not every one who says to me "Lord, Lord" shall enter the kingdom of heaven, but the one who does the will of my Father who is in heaven. On that day (of judgment) many will say to me, "Lord, Lord, did we not prophesy in your name, and cast out demons in your name, and do mighty works in your name?" And then I will declare to them, "I never knew you; depart from me you evildoers." (Mt 7.21–23)

Though good works, including prophecies and miracles, may be done without love, the love of faithful Christians must still be realized in good works. Christians prove their faith and love for God in concrete acts of mercy such as those described in Christ's parable of the final judgment: feeding the hungry, giving drink to the thirsty, clothing the naked, sheltering the homeless, and visiting and caring for the infirm and imprisoned (Mt 25.35–36). This is the apostolic teaching found in the writings of James and John and Paul.

If a brother or sister is ill-clad and in lack of daily food, and one of you says to them, "Go in peace, be warmed and filled," without giving them the things needed for the body, what does it profit? So faith by itself, if it has no works is dead. (Jas 2.15–17)

By this we know love, that he laid down his life for us; and we ought to lay down our lives for the brethren. But if any one has the world's goods and sees his brother in need, yet closes his heart against him, how does God's love abide in him? Little children, let us not love in word or speech but in deed and in truth. (1 Jn 3.17–18)

If I have prophetic powers and understand all mysteries and all knowledge, and if I have all faith, so as to remove mountains, but have not love, I am nothing. If I give away all that I have (to the poor), and if I deliver my body to be burned, but have not love, I gain nothing. (1 Cor 13.2–3)

When Christians believe and love God in his Son Jesus, they keep all of God's laws that are summed up in the two great commandments, to love God and the neighbor (cf. Lk 10.25–37). Christ insists that God's commandments are good and light and not at all burdensome (Mt 11.28–30).[2] This is because they are accomplished not by human strength, which is impossible, but by God's grace. When people live in love with faith in God, and by God's grace, they use all their talents and gifts, endure all their troubles and trials, and suffer all their pains and losses for God's glory and the good of others. They do this by the Holy Spirit's indwelling power. They strive in every way to attain "the fruit of the Spirit" described by St Paul as "love, joy, peace, patience, kindness, goodness, faithfulness, gentleness, and self-control" (Gal 5.22). In a word, again quoting St Paul, they become "imitators of God" (Eph 5.1).

God's People, Christ's Body, Spirit's Temple

Christianity is an imitation of God. The church fathers and saints repeat this conviction in many different ways. Sometimes they go so far as to say that faithful Christians not only imitate and resemble God in keeping his commandments and teachings, but that they participate directly in God's own being and life by his divine energies given in Christ and

---

[2]The English translation of the passage where Christ speaks of his yoke being "easy" might be more accurately translated *good* rather than *easy* (Mt 11.30). The word is the same used in Psalm 34.8: "O taste and see that the Lord is *good*."

the Holy Spirit. The saints testify that in and through Christ and the Holy Spirit, believing Christians become divine by grace. They become, through God's gracious goodwill, all that Christ himself is. They become literally divine, while remaining human. They become God's own people, Christ's body and the Holy Spirit's temple in the world.[3]

The fundamental self-identification of Christians, therefore, before everything else, is as members of Christ and members of Christ's Body, the Church. Before everything else, Christians see themselves as temples of God's Holy Spirit. They strive to be the "called and chosen and faithful" people (cf. Rev 17.14) who belong to the Lord and find their being and life solely in him. This is witnessed in the Holy Scriptures in many different ways. St Paul, for example, says:

> Do you not know that your bodies are members of Christ? (1 Cor 6.15)

> Do you not know that your body is a temple of the Holy Spirit within you, which you have from God? You are not your own; you were bought with a price. (1 Cor 6.19)

> Now there are a variety of gifts, but the same Spirit; and there are varieties of service, but the same Lord; and there are varieties of working, but it is the same God who inspires them all in every one. To each is given the manifestation of the Spirit for the common good. (1 Cor 12.4–7)

> For just as the body is one and has many members, and all the members of the body, though many, are one body, so it is with Christ. For by one Spirit we were all baptized into one body (. . .) and all were made to drink of one Spirit. For the body does not consist of one member, but of many. (1 Cor 12.12–14)

> Now you are the body of Christ and individually members of it. (1 Cor 12.27)

---

[3]In addition to the biblical images of the Church as God's people with Christ as the New Adam; Christ's Body of which he is the head; and the Holy Spirit's temple of which Christ is the chief cornerstone, other scriptural images are used for the Church. These include the Church as God's kingdom ruled by Christ who reigns as God's only Son, having served as God's only slave; God's household where God the Father's unique Son Christ heads the assembly of those who become God's children in, with, and through him; God's flock tended by Christ the Good Shepherd and Lamb; the vineyard that God's right hand has planted, with Christ being the vine and the believers the branches (Ps 80.14–15, Jn 15.1–7); the virgin Bride of Christ the Bridegroom (Eph 5.21–33, 2 Cor 11.2, Rev 21); and God's army led by Christ the Lamb who conquers (Rev *passim*, Eph 6.10–17) Orthodox liturgy abounds with references to all of these images and symbols.

Another Pauline epistle puts the same teaching in this way:

> There is one body and one Spirit . . . one Lord, one faith, one baptism, one
> God and Father of us all who is above all and through all and in all. But
> grace was given to each of us according to the measure of Christ's gift.
>
> And his gifts were that some should be apostles, some prophets, some
> evangelists, some pastors and teachers, to equip the saints for the work
> of ministry, for building up the body of Christ until we all attain to the
> unity of the faith and of the knowledge of the Son of God, to mature man-
> hood, to the measure of the stature of the fullness of Christ . . .
>
> . . . speaking the truth in love, we are to grow up in every way into
> him who is the head, into Christ, from whom the whole body, joined and
> knit together by every joint with which it is supplied, when each part is
> working properly, makes bodily growth and upbuilds itself in love.
> (Eph 4.4–16)

In the first of two letters ascribed to St Peter it is said like this:

> Come to him, to that living stone, rejected by men but in God's sight cho-
> sen and precious; and like living stones be yourselves built into a spiri-
> tual house, to be a holy priesthood, to offer spiritual sacrifices acceptable
> to God through Jesus Christ. . . .
>
> . . . (for) you are a chosen race, a royal priesthood, a holy nation, God's
> own people (or a people for God's own possession), that you may declare
> the wonderful deeds of him who called you out of darkness into his mar-
> velous light. Once you were no people; but now you are God's people;
> once you had not received mercy but now you have received mercy. (1 Pet
> 2.4–5,9–10)

Laity and Clergy

As witnessed in earliest Christian history beginning with the canonical New Testament Scriptures, the Christian Church as God's people,
Christ's Body and the Holy Spirit's temple (as well as God's kingdom,
household, flock, vineyard, bride, and army) was understood to be the
entire community of baptized believers. Within this community a
small number of men and women possessing very specific qualifications, after being identified and tested, received a second "laying on of
hands" (*cheirotonia*) to be a bishop, presbyter, male or female deacon,
or (in the earliest church) an enrolled widow[4] (cf. Phil 1.1, 1 and 2 Tim

---

[4]The word "bishop" translates the Greek *episkopos*, which literally means "supervi-
sor" or "overseer." It was the name for the chief steward or servant in a household who

and Titus). These church members received the "laying on of hands" for their official ecclesial ministries by the will of God and the grace of the Holy Spirit, through the consent of the whole community. They existed then, and continue to exist now (except for deaconesses and enrolled widows), to serve the *pleroma* (fullness) of the faithful in very specific ways.

The bishops were to oversee their communities in all aspects of their life and work. They were to preach and teach the Word of God, to preside over the celebration of the Christian mysteries (or sacraments), especially baptisms (including chrismations, i.e. the sealing of the baptized with the gift of the Holy Spirit), and eucharistic liturgies. They were to instruct, edify, guide, inspire, correct, and console the faithful. Guarding "what had been entrusted to them by the Holy Spirit (the *paratheke* or *depositum*)" (1 Tim 6.20, 2 Tim 1.14) and "rightly handling the word of truth" (2 Tim 2.15), they were to "set the believers an example in speech and conduct, in love, in faith, in purity" (1 Tim 4.11). Being charged through the apostolic laying on of hands to "tend the flock of God . . . not by constraint but willingly, not for shameful gain but eagerly, not as domineering over those in (their) charge but being examples to the flock" (1 Pet 5.1–3), they were to do everything possible to assist and empower all members of their churches to be genuine Christians in all aspects of their personal, ecclesial, social, political, and professional lives.

The bishops also represented their particular churches to other churches and in mutual meetings. They had the duty to examine, test, and ordain the new bishops of other churches in their regions. As God's chief steward and servant in a community of stewards and servants, the bishops (and later the presbyters ordained and assigned by them) had,

spoke in the master's name and exercised the master's authority, but was not the master himself. The word "presbyter" translates the Greek *presbyteros*, which simply means "old man" or "elder." The word "deacon" translates the Greek *diakonos*, which means "servant" or "minister." It is used in New Testament writings for both men and women. According to the New Testament Scriptures, one of the several qualifications for serving in the church as a bishop or presbyter was to be a single or once-married man. Male deacons also had to be single or once-married. Women deacons and enrolled widows also had to have been only once-married; with the married women deacons serving in the church only after their children were raised. On the issue of women in the diaconate, see the article by Kyriaki Karidoyanes Fitzgerald, "The Nature and Characteristics of the Order of Deaconess," in *Women and the Priesthood*, Thomas Hopko, ed., Revised Edition (Crestwood, N.Y.: SVS Press, 1999), 93–137.

and continue still to have, this one essential purpose: to preserve, guard, guarantee, and enhance the unity, identity, integrity, fidelity, solidarity, conciliarity, and continuity of their particular church, and so to ensure that each of them, always and everywhere, would be truly the same one, holy, catholic, and apostolic Church of God and Christ in every aspect of its being and life.

The bishops were, and still are, assisted in their ministry by the presbyters and deacons. They are also assisted by members of the Body with particular charismatic gifts from God, such as teaching, prophesying, evangelizing, administering, healing, interceding, and miracle-working. Eventually bishops assigned presbyters (who came to be called "priests") to function under their authority as leaders of smaller or distant Christian communities. The presbyters then began themselves to preach and teach God's Word, to preside at the celebration of the Christian mysteries (or sacraments), and to govern the life and work of their communities, of which they were, as heads, the leading members.

In all the churches there were also deacons, both men and women, who assisted in the sacramental and philanthropic work of the community. Later there came to be other ecclesial ministries such as subdeacon, reader, singer, taper-bearer, doorkeeper, catechist, and exorcist. There were also, as we already noted, charismatic ministries performed by both men and women, including the roles of prophet, teacher, healer, miracle-worker, counselor, and administrator. Eventually there emerged monastic communities of various kinds for both men and women, originating, it seems, from the early orders of widows and virgins.

Most important for us to see today, and to understand clearly, is that the Church of God and Christ is the whole *pleroma* of the faithful, not just the ordained clergy. God's people and Christ's Body and the Holy Spirit's temple, theologically, spiritually, and canonically, always denotes the Church as a whole, never only the small number of the baptized who are ordained as bishops, presbyters, and deacons for service to the whole body of baptized believers.

We must note as well that the term *laity*, as used today in contrast to the ordained *clergy*, derives from the term *laos*, which means *people*. It originally meant the entire body of the faithful, including the *clergy*. The word *clergy (kleros)*, now means *those who have been set aside* for a particular service in the Church; but it originally referred to

the entire Church as that portion (*kleronomia*) of the human race
called, chosen, and set apart to be "a chosen race, a royal priesthood, a
holy nation, God's own people" (1 Peter 2.9), to stand before God on
behalf all peoples and nations (cf. Rev 1.5–6). When we now speak of
"clergy and laity," or "the clergy and the people," we can do so without misconceptions only if we know the etymology of the words, the
changes of language, and also therefore, the changes of understanding,
that have occurred historically. If we fail to do this, we will erroneously
identify the Church with the clergy alone, as, alas, so many people
today so often do.

Clergy and Laity in History

We must also realize that the Church has undergone many changes in
the course of history. Beginning as rather small groups of believers in
city churches headed by one bishop, with presbyters and deacons, the
Christian Church was established as the official religion of the Roman-
Byzantine Empire at the end of the fourth century. At that time the
bishops began to govern large territories of people with, eventually, just
about everyone being a member of the Christian Church, however
nominally and formally. This changed things radically. The laity at this
time included emperors and civil authorities in an earthly political
entity (*politeuma*), whose flag was the double-headed eagle. The *laos*
and the *kleronomia* of God and of Christ became the empire itself, and
not simply the Church.

The empire ended with the subjugation of the eastern Christian
churches and peoples by the Ottoman Muslims. During this period of
nearly five hundred years of Turkish rule (*tourkokratia*), the bishops
were given civil powers over the Christian laity. They collected taxes,
controlled behavior, judged disputes, and generally were answerable for
the actions of their people to the Turkish rulers. Because they were
appointed by the Ottoman rulers, the leading bishops throughout the
Ottoman Empire were of Greek nationality, as, for example, are the
bishops of the Patriarchate of Jerusalem to this day. The Orthodox peoples of Serbia, Bulgaria, Romania, and Albania remember this period
only too well.

The bishops under Ottoman control also adopted all of the insignia
of the Christian lay rulers of the former empire. They wore the Turkish

judicial robe (*riasson*). They carried staffs and stood on eagle rugs and sat on the thrones formerly used by imperial civil authorities. They grew long hair, which was a sign of secular power in the Christian empire in which the clergy's hair was tonsured. They wore imperial crowns in church, and the imperial vestment (*sakkos*.) In a word, the bishops, and by extension the clergy, became rulers over the total life of the Christian laity, the majority of whose strong and clever young men were taken by the Turks as janissaries. This, too, created a radical change in the relationship between clergy and laity in the Church.

The Church in the Russian Empire had a different destiny. Escaping subjugation by Islam, the Russian Orthodox Church was subjugated to the Westernizing and secularizing imperial policies begun by Peter the Great in the beginning of the eighteenth century. The patriarchate was abolished and the Church was administered after the pattern of the Reformed Church in Holland, controlled by state authority in the person of the Ober-procurator of the Holy Synod. When the Russian Church in the seventeenth century adopted the ways of the Church under Ottoman rule, including the rituals and dress, a schism occurred in which up to a third of the faithful, called the "Old Believers" or "Old-Ritualists," dissented from the established Church. This schismatic body considered Peter and his successors to be anti-Christs. The official clergy during the imperial period were tightly controlled. Their publications and sermons were censured. The majority of the faithful were uneducated and illiterate. The clergy became a caste who lived off their people, not having a salary until the end of the nineteenth century. The upper classes were secularized. So, the relationship between clergy and laity in the church was radically altered: on the highest levels of hierarchs and aristocrats, and on the popular levels of parish priests and peasants.

Then there was the short interlude of the emergence of national states and churches in the Balkans, characterized by severe tensions in virtually all churches with the Phanar, that is, ecclesiastical leadership of the former Ottoman period. This was a time of the birth of the violent, even virulent, nationalism among all the Orthodox peoples of the region that still plagues our churches—and that again affects the relationship of clergy and laity.

Then communism came, first to the Russian empire and then to the Balkan nations.

The Marxist period, during which the churches were enslaved and persecuted and leaders were imprisoned and murdered, created another abnormal situation between the government controlled and appointed clergy (and those who hid and dissented from the official church) and the remnant of believing Christian laity.

Disentangling this complex history, and making application to contemporary church life and mission—and especially to the relationship between clergy and laity in all the Orthodox churches today—is a daunting task that competent, dispassionate people have hardly begun to debate seriously and systematically. This is certainly the case in regard to the issue of church governance, which in North America has been further complicated by manifold influences of the "American way of life": democratic rule, individual rights, corporate rights, property rights, separation of church and state, parishes as voluntary societies and civil corporations, parishes as ethnic and cultural centers, and the relationship between the so-called *diaspora* churches here in North America and their mother churches in the "old country."

Having this overview of the Body of Christ and a superficial history of the Orthodox churches allows us to envisage the work of Orthodox laity in their churches and in society, particularly in America. In trying to understand and apply this vision, a special word must be said about Christian monks and nuns, and about those who cannot work because of sickness and disability.

Clergy and Laity in the Contemporary Church

Christian laypeople must identify and present themselves first of all as Christians, as members of the Christian Church; the people, family, and household of God; the Body and Bride of Christ; the temple and dwelling-place of the Holy Spirit. The question is crucial: Do laypeople experience themselves primarily as people created, redeemed, sanctified, and deified by God through Christ and the Holy Spirit? Or, do they think that experience is only for ordained clergy?

The first and basic task of Christian laypeople is to maintain and develop themselves as creatures made in God's image and likeness, who have died and risen with Christ in baptism, and have been anointed and sealed by God's Holy Spirit. They must participate in the eucharistic sacrifice of Jesus the Messiah to God his Father. They must acknowledge themselves as not being their own, but belonging to God. They must delight in the fact, to use Fr Alexander Schmemann's celebrated formula, that before anything else they are "doxological and eucharistic beings" whose reason for being is to give glory and thanksgiving to God for his mighty and merciful acts.

Laypeople find and fulfill their lives in the Church under the guidance and direction of the clergy. The bishops and priests, with the assistance of the deacons and others exercising church ministries and charismatic callings, serve the laypeople by helping them to do God's work, according the God's will, in obedience to God's Word. In apostolic words, the clergy exist to "equip the saints for the work of (their) ministry" (Eph 4.10).

The clergy gather the laypeople together. They proclaim the gospel to them. They teach them God's Word. They instruct them in the Christian faith. They baptize and chrismate them and their children. They preside at their eucharistic meals. They lead them in liturgical worship. They assist them in discerning their callings in life. They help them to make decisions in their daily lives. They correct them when they go astray. They support them in their temptations and trials. They are with them in their illnesses and sorrows. They care for them when they die. And they intercede and advocate for them before God from before their birth, throughout their lives, and after their departure from this earth.

Besides practicing their own charismatic ministries within the Body of Christ, laypeople are to support the clergy in the performance of their duties. They are also to insist that their leaders do their duties well. Laypeople help the clergy first of all by providing them with proper education and training. They also ensure that they have adequate salaries, housing, facilities, equipment, and resources to do their work. Lay Christians also serve the clergy by inviting and welcoming their leadership, and by offering their prayers, encouragement, and support. They also serve by questioning and correcting them when they see that they are failing to fulfill their duties properly. They do this in a positive and gentle manner in their regular interaction with them on a daily basis. They do so as well with a strong and vibrant sense of their mutual responsibility together for the life and work of the Church.

The Church, as we have seen, is a conciliar body. It is the entire assembly of the faithful. Nothing is to be done in the Church, since nothing can be done in a godly and truly Christian and churchly manner, without the leadership and guidance of the clergy. But, in turn, the clergy must acknowledge and confess that they can do nothing without the laypeople. The laypeople are accountable to the clergy, and, in turn, the clergy are accountable to the laypeople. Because of the very nature of Christian life, there is no division between religious and secular, spiritual and material, clerical and lay. Everything is done in and for God, and by God's grace and power, by all of the members of the Body working together, each doing his or her part, according to his or her place, calling, and ministry within the one Body.

Dealing with Ecclesiastical Disputes

The Church's canons provide guidelines and procedures for dealing with laypeople who persist in unchristian attitudes and actions. They also provide guidelines and procedures for dealing with bishops, priests, and deacons who transgress church teaching and practice, and so fail to fulfill their ministries. Finding the proper interpretation of these canons for contemporary issues in the Church, and applying them properly and justly, are among the greatest challenges in Orthodoxy today.

When dealing with failings in the Church, and disputes about duties and ministries and rights and properties, one thing should be clear. Christians are never to turn to civil powers or secular judgments to resolve their ecclesial disagreements. If even for members of the Church "to have lawsuits at all with one another," as St Paul already writes to the first Christians, "is defeat for you," how much more of a "defeat" is it when lawsuits occur between clergy and laity in the Church, or between parishes, dioceses, and churches? "Why not suffer wrong? Why not yourself be defrauded?" asks Christ's apostle? (1 Cor 6.1–8). God will vindicate the righteous. Christ alone is our advocate and our judge. The many lawsuits and court cases in and between Orthodox churches in North America in recent decades sadly attests to this truth already testified to in apostolic Scripture. The only winner in any court case between Christians and churches is the devil.[5]

[5]When Christians, lay or clergy, are accused of criminal actions, recourse to criminal courts is obligatory. Our issue here is solely about disputes among Christians concerning church matters being resolved by civil suits rather than by ecclesiastical courts.

When members of the Church believe that they are not receiving a just and loving response to their legitimate requests and grievances, their sole recourse is to appeal to higher ecclesial authorities. They appeal from priest to dean to bishop to archbishop to synod in search of resolution and satisfaction. When all appeals fail, the only recourse left to believing Christians, clergy or lay, is to appeal to God, to confess the Christian faith and to endure in their convictions with forgiveness to those who inflict injustice and suffering upon them. God will vindicate his people whose cause is just and true, either in this world, or in the age to come. What must never happen is that evil be returned for evil, or that unchristian attitudes and actions (including recourse to civil rights or secular courts or political principles) be brought into Christian Church affairs. The Church is neither a democracy nor a hierocracy. Its members, clergy and laypeople, have no powers or rights. They have only gifts and services. They conquer only by truth and love in sacrificial suffering with their crucified Christ, their sole Savior and Judge.

Lay Ministries in the Church

When things are working properly in the church, many ministries can be performed by laity in and for the ecclesial community. Laypeople receive gifts from God for many services that build up the church and edify, instruct, inspire, encourage, and comfort the faithful. Some of these services in times past, like reading, singing, and serving at liturgical services, teaching people the Christian faith, visiting the sick and imprisoned, caring for the poor and needy, and administering church properties and resources, were done by the clergy. The ordained deacons, both women and men, were especially involved in administering the daily life of the church and doing good works under the guidance of bishops and priests. Today, any baptized man or woman with the competence to perform these services may be blessed by their bishop or priest to do them, without a formal rite of ordination or appointment. This is especially true today in areas of pastoral care, psychological counseling, and spiritual guidance and assistance. It is also true in areas of church administration and finance.

Essential elements in ministry are charism, calling, and competence. A sad and seriously harmful "trivialization" of Christian faith and life occurs when men, women, and sometimes even young people and children—ordained and not ordained—are allowed to do things in church without ability or competence.

While there are many ministries that Christian laity can and must do in and for the church, the Christian men and women who comprise the great majority of the faithful do their Christian work primarily at home and in society. They express their faith and love for God in good deeds done in their families, in acts of mercy to friends and neighbors, and in the daily work that they do in their jobs and professions.

God's Work in the Home

Doing God's work at home is the same for clergy and laity. It consists in parents loving each other and caring for their children in the obvious ways: spiritually, intellectually, emotionally, and physically. It consists in children honoring their parents with proper obedience, respect and care.

The first of one's neighbors to be loved are the members of one's own natural household. "Charity begins at home" is an apostolic teaching. "If anyone does not provide for his relatives, and especially for his own family, he has disowned the faith and is worse than an unbeliever" (1 Tim 5.8).

While some who call themselves Christians may sin by failing to care for their own flesh and blood—being rude and negligent at home while acting politely and kindly to those outside—others may sin by idolizing their families—including their countries, nations, and churches—and by failing to care seriously for anyone other than "their own." Such communities can assume ultimate value in people's lives and become objects of idolatrous worship. It is imperative to remember the radical teaching of Christ that "he who loves father or mother more than me is not worthy of me; and he who loves son or daughter more than me is not worthy of me; and he who does not take up his cross and follow me is not worthy of me" (Mt 10.37–38). In St Luke's Gospel Jesus' hyperbolic rhetoric is even more extreme when he says "if anyone comes to me and does not hate his own father and mother and wife and children and brothers and sisters, yes, and even his own life (*psyche*), he cannot be my disciple" (Lk 14.26).

God's Work in the World

The main arena for Christian laity to do good deeds and provide helpful services in Christ's name is not found in the churches nor even in the "small churches" of their households. It is found rather in their daily life and work outside their homes and churches. Christian laypeople work in the world. Christian clergy are forbidden to do so, except when they might have to take certain jobs that do not compromise or harm their ecclesial ministries in order to support themselves and their families, and sometimes even their churches. Thus, for example, Christian clergymen may not be politicians, lawyers, judges, businessmen, bankers, or soldiers. They may, however, be farmers and physicians, and, in some cases, teachers, counselors, and social workers.

Christian laypeople, unlike the clergy, do their Christian work primarily in society. They express their faith and love for God in service to their neighbors in and through their daily work. On the Day of Judgment Christian men and women will give an account to God and their fellow creatures, not only for their church activity, personal piety, and family behavior. They also will answer for what they did with their daily lives and what they did for other people in their jobs and professions. And, they will be required to defend how they did it.

Christian laity, like Christian clergy, will be asked if they behaved in a godly manner, if they kept God's commandments, if they acquired the fruit of God's Spirit in everyday activities. They will be asked if they acknowledged their sins and faults, and worked to overcome them. They will be asked if they dealt lovingly, justly, and honestly with other people, with patience, kindness, gentleness, and purity. They will be asked if they were poor in spirit and pure in heart, and meek and merciful, working to make peace and mourning over evil, sickness, suffering, and death. Additionally, they will be asked how they performed their actual work.

Physicians, for example, will give an account of their professional work, as will teachers, lawyers, judges, politicians, business people, social workers, scientists, artists, athletes, law enforcement officers, and military men and women. Doctors, to pursue our example, will not simply be asked if they were honest and kind and patient with their patients. Still less will they be merely asked if they went to church on Sunday, served on the parish council, sung in the choir, hung an icon on their office wall, and put Christian literature in their waiting rooms. They will be asked, first and foremost, how they performed their work. Did they treat those who came to them as competently as they could? Did they make every effort to do so? Did they keep up with the latest healing techniques, treatments, and medications? Were they skillful and responsible in their diagnoses and procedures and prescriptions? Did they care about those who came to be cured? Did they sin by using their positions, powers, and skills negligently, or merely for personal profit or prestige, or, even worse, for plainly wicked, destructive, or death-dealing purposes?

The examples can be multiplied. Were teachers, prepared with the best pedagogical skills and resources, effective in teaching their teachable students? Were scientists careful in their experiments, competent in dealing with their data, and accurate in their research and reporting? Were artists—or workers or farmers or technicians—respectful of their material, diligent in their craft, disciplined in their performance, pure in their production, true in their creativity? Were lawyers and judges competent in their knowledge of the laws and just in their application and administration? Were police and military men and women steadfast in using their power to defend the innocent and to cause the least possible pain to the guilty? Were business people honest in their dealings, making the best possible products and providing the best possible services at the lowest possible cost to their customers?

We need not continue with more examples. The point should be clear. Christian laity, like the clergy, express their faith and love for God and their fellow human beings in their daily work. At the Lord's judgment they will give account for what they did in their jobs and professions, and how they did it. For, as Scripture repeatedly teaches, the Lord will "render to every person according to his work(s)." (Ps 62.12; Prov 24.12; Rom 2.6; Rev 22.12) And, as Scripture also teaches, the Lord will save all human works and acts in ways known to himself. Nothing that we creatures have done or made that is good and true and beautiful will be lost. This age will pass away, and everything in it. But everything that is precious in God's sight will be saved. This is God's gospel in Jesus.

Suffering Laity and Monastics

Christians will have to answer before God for how they have dealt with life's injustices and afflictions. They will have to account for how they have handled their weaknesses, losses, and failures. Some Christian laypeople may have nothing to offer to God and their fellows, and nothing to answer for in life but what they have had to endure in their earthly existence. They will have been unable to work as others do because of ill health and disabilities of mind and body. They will have done virtually nothing but suffer, being unable to work in any way at all. Some may spend years of their lives, and even their entire lifetimes, being served and cared for by others. This is surely so, for example, in the cases of people born with severe illnesses. To have such a calling from God, or to be a parent or close relative of a person with this calling, may well be the most difficult and honored of all human vocations, the greatest of all human "works." It is certainly the calling closest to that of Christ who came to bear our injustices, endure our wounds, share our sorrows, carry our sins, and die our deaths in order to heal, save, and sanctify us and the whole of creation.

Christians whom God calls to the monastic life have no specific work to do in church or society. Except for the monks ordained to serve in monastic churches, monastic Christians are laypeople. We are not speaking here of the men who serve as bishops and priests who do not live the monastic life strictly speaking, and perhaps never have done so, though they are clothed and tonsured as monks and may keep some forms of monastic discipline in their personal lives. Nor are we speaking of the laypeople who, for whatever reasons, are blessed to wear monastic clothing and even to receive the monastic tonsure, who live outside monasteries.

Monastic Christians live under obedience to their elders in communal monasteries, sketes, and hermitages. They are celibate, poor, and free from all churchly and societal cares and duties. They serve God and their fellow humans, and, indeed, the whole of creation, through their ascetical feats of fighting sinful passions through silence, fasting, vigil, and prayer. They are intentionally engaged in constant warfare against every form of wickedness in and with Jesus Christ "the Son of God who appeared to destroy the works of the devil" (1 Jn 3.9). They are victorious in their good works by God's grace through their regular work of psalmody, hymnody, petition, intercession, supplication, thanksgiving, and praise. They serve the people whom God brings to them as God demands and allows, treating every person as Christ himself. They model proper care for God's creation and proper use of God's gifts. They demonstrate the spiritual significance of everything material, and the material significance of everything spiritual. They provide edification, encouragement, and comfort to everyone without condition, asking nothing in return. They function as living canons of faith, hope, and love for all people—beginning with their fellow Christians, who are not to imitate the external forms of their monastic life, but rather to follow their spiritual example within the conditions of their own life and work.

All Working Together for God

In conclusion, we see that all baptized believers constitute the Christian Church. All are God's people. All are members of Christ's Body. All are temples of the Holy Spirit. The ordained clergy lead and govern the churches as "servants of the servants of God," who are called, trained, and ordained to assist all members of the Church in finding and fulfilling their calling as Christians. The monks and nuns have their special witness and work; so do those blessed by God to suffer sickness and infirmity. The great majority of Christians, however, the Christian laity, serve God and neighbor primarily at home and in their everyday work in the world. May each one of us find our place and do our work, in communion with all others, to the glory of God and for the good of all.

Eucharistic Discipline in the Orthodox Church[1]

P eople of whatever convictions—theistic or atheistic, Christian or non-Christian—who behave in an orderly and respectful manner may attend liturgical services in an Orthodox church, and participate, as far as possible, in the prayers and rituals (such as singing psalms and hymns, and venerating icons and relics). But only members of the Orthodox Church who practice a specific spiritual discipline may participant in the Church's sacraments and receive Holy Communion at the Orthodox eucharistic liturgies. The essential elements of eucharistic discipline in the Orthodox Church may be simply stated in five points.

1 Participation in Holy Communion in the Orthodox Church requires first of all that a person be a baptized, chrismated member of the Orthodox Church, who fully accepts the conditions and demands of his or her baptism and chrismation. Eucharistic discipline in the Orthodox Church demands that communicants in the eucharistic sacrifice understand themselves at all times and in all circumstances as having died and risen with Christ, as being sealed by the Holy Spirit, and as belonging to God as his bonded servants and free-born sons in Jesus.

2 Baptism and chrismation, and so, participation in Holy Communion, requires a person to believe in the Word of God, the gospel of Christ, and the Christian faith summarized in the Nicene-Constantinopolitan Creed, as these are proclaimed and interpreted in the Orthodox Church. Members of the Orthodox Church who question biblical or churchly doctrines may participate in Holy Communion

---

[1]This short statement was made for Orthodox Education Day at St Vladimir's Seminary in October 1999.

if they are praying and working to come to an enlightened understanding of the Orthodox faith under the guidance of their pastors
and teachers. Those who have been baptized and chrismated in the
Orthodox Church who publicly express doubt and disbelief about
the faith as confessed and lived in the Orthodox Church, or secretly
harbor such doubt and disbelief, may not partake of Holy Communion at Orthodox eucharistic liturgies.

3 Confessing the Christian faith as understood and practiced in the
Orthodox Church is to identify fully with Orthodox Church history
and tradition, and to take full responsibility for it. It is to accept and
defend the dogmas and canons of the councils accepted by the Orthodox Churches, to worship according to Orthodox liturgical rites, to
venerate those who are glorified as Orthodox saints, and to struggle
to practice the ethical and moral teachings of Christ and his apostles
as recorded in the holy scriptures and elaborated in Orthodox
Church tradition. Because participation in the holy Eucharist is not
only a sacred communion with God through Christ and the Holy
Spirit, but also a Holy Communion with Orthodox believers of all
times and places, responsibility for the whole of Orthodox Church
history and tradition is an absolute condition for partaking in the
Holy Communion of Christ's Body and Blood at the Church's
eucharistic liturgies.

4 Identifying fully with Orthodox Christian teaching and practice
requires a communicant in the Orthodox Church to strive to put the
Church's biblical, evangelical, and apostolic teachings into practice
daily. No one can believe and do everything perfectly. Eucharistic
discipline, however, demands that a communicant struggles to do so,
admitting when he or she fails, and repenting without self-justifica-
tion over failures and sins. This means concretely that eucharistic
discipline requires a communicant—as far as possible—to study
God's Word in Scripture, to pray and fast and give alms, to attend
church services regularly, and to live according to God's commandments in all aspects of life and work, regularly giving an account to
a spiritual authority recognized by the Church, repenting of sins, and
struggling by God's grace to change and improve. Persons rejecting
such a disciplined life may not partake of Holy Communion in the
Orthodox Church.

5 Eucharistic discipline in the Orthodox Church finally requires that a communicant be in constant repentance, realizing that he or she is never deserving of receiving Holy Communion, and knowing that the heartfelt confession of one's unworthiness is an absolute condition for partaking in a worthy manner. The essential expression and vital acknowledgement of one's unworthiness to receive Christ's Body and Blood in Holy Communion, together with the confession of one's sins, is the forgiveness of other people. Eucharistic discipline demands that communicants of Christ's Body and Blood be at peace with everyone as far as they can be, even when others are unwilling to forgive and be reconciled with them. At least within themselves, partakers of Holy Communion at an Orthodox Divine Liturgy must be in a union of love with all people, including their worst enemies.

Acceptance of one's baptism and chrismation in the Church, responsibility for the Church's faith and life, the struggle to put the faith fully into practice, accountability for personal belief and behavior, constant and continual repentance, and peace with all people in the union of love commanded and given by God in Christ and the Holy Spirit—these are the requirements for participation in Holy Communion in the Orthodox Church. They are, ultimately and essentially, what Holy Communion is all about.

The Unity We Still Seek[1]

The unity that Christians of apostolic faith and tradition still seek for their churches is the unity of Christ with God the Father in the Holy Spirit. According to St John's Gospel, Jesus prayed for this unity for his apostles and for those who would believe in him through their word. He prayed for this unity so that the world might know and believe that the God who loves and sends him also loves and sends those whom he loves and sends, with all those who believe through their teaching (Jn 17.1–26). All creation is made for this divine unity. Israel, God's first-born son, bears it to the nations. Jesus, the Messiah of Israel and the unique Son of God, is crucified and glorified that it may be accomplished. The Holy Spirit is given that it may be fulfilled.

Christ's unity with God the Father in the Holy Spirit, a unity eternally existing in the Uncreated Trinity, is manifested on earth where God acts through his Word and Spirit with his creatures, whether or not they consciously know it. This unity is being realized where men and women strive for truth, love, justice, peace, beauty, joy, and all the divine qualities for which they, being in God's image and likeness, are made. To the measure that human beings seek God's perfection and cooperate with God's grace, knowingly or unknowingly, there will be unity, communion, and life. To the degree that they doubt and deny their divine destiny, there will be division and death.

The Church of Christ

From an Orthodox Christian perspective, God has already united all things in Christ. He has already made his Son the head over all things. This is God's plan before the foundation of the ages. It is the "mystery

---

[1]This is a revision of a paper delivered at a conference on ecumenism held at the Tantur Ecumenical Center in Israel in Spring 1997. For the original version, with the other papers from the conference, see *Ecumenism, Present Realities and Future Prospects*, Lawrence S. Cunningham, Ed. (Indiana: Notre Dame, 1998).

of Christ," hidden from the angels and made known in the Church, which, according to apostolic testimony, is the Israel of God, Christ's Body and Bride, the temple of the Holy Spirit, the pillar and bulwark of the truth, the fullness of him who fills all in all.[2] The sole reason for the Church's being is to make Christ's unity with God in the Spirit knowable and accessible to humanity until Jesus returns in glory to establish divine unity in the universe.

The Church, as Fr Alexander Schmemann[3] has said, is not an organization with a gospel; it is a gospel with organizations; it is not an institution with mysteries; it is a mystery with institutions. Church unity, in this perspective, is unity in the gospel of God and the mystery of Christ as revealed, known, proclaimed, celebrated, and witnessed in the formal ecclesial doctrines, sacramental structures, and liturgical rites of the Christian churches. In this perspective, Church unity has virtually nothing to do with theological systems, church politics, popular pieties, or holy people. It has only to do with the formal faith, order, and worship of the Christian churches *qua churches*. It is about what the churches of Christ, as Christ's one holy Church, believe, teach, pray, and do.[4] Theologians and theological systems come and go; so do ecclesiastical policies and actions and pietistic devotions and practices. Some are formally received and canonized, thereby becoming part of the Church's divine humanity in history. Others are dismissed and forgotten. Still others produce factions and divisions, schisms, and heresies.

Righteous people, some graced with extraordinary sanctity, are found everywhere, within the churches and without. God is not bound. His divine Word, incarnate as Jesus Christ, fashions everyone and everything. His quickening Spirit, everywhere present, blows where he wills. The Lord acts in and with all of his creatures according to their willingness and ability to cooperate with his divine energies. God builds communion and unity wherever, however, and in whomever he can.

These Orthodox Christian convictions stand, because God acts personally and directly within human history through his divine Word and

---

[2]See Rom 11; Gal 6; 1 Cor 3,6,12; 1 Tim 3; Eph 1,4; Rev 21.

[3]Protopresbyter Alexander Schmemann, Dean of St Vladimir's Orthodox Theological Seminary from 1962 to 1983 and a leading Orthodox theologian, died in 1983 at the age of 62.

[4]Cf. Georges Florovsky, "Primitive Tradition and the Traditions," in *The Unity We Seek: Lectures on the Church and the Churches* (Toronto, 1962).

Spirit in his chosen people. He founds his new and final covenant community with his creatures on faith in his Son Jesus, the Messiah of Israel, so that the fullness of grace and truth, of unity and communion, of life and beatitude, and, indeed, of Divinity itself, may be fully present and consciously known by human beings, from the least to the greatest, who believe and are baptized. God establishes his Church and acts within it so that he may truly be "all and in all" for those who know and love him, or rather more accurately, who are known and loved by him, in Jesus Christ and the Holy Spirit.

Faith, Order, and Worship

The unity that apostolic Christians seek for the churches is the unity that is actualized wherever God acts among creatures. It is the communion with God that Christian saints consciously know and experience. It is the Church's unity in faith, order, and worship, which, according to the *Acts of the Apostles,* is finally and fully given to Christ's disciples on the day of Pentecost after the Lord's Passover.

Still, this unity, ideally portrayed in *Acts,* scarcely existed among all who claimed to be disciples of Jesus. According to the Christian Scriptures, controversies and disputes about Jesus existed among the various Jewish parties and the first Gentile Christians. There were always factions and divisions (*haireseis* and *schismata*) that were, according to St Paul—himself a greatly disputed figure—inevitable and even necessary "so that the genuine among you may be recognized" (*ina oi dokimoi phaneroi genontai en hymin*) (1 Cor 11.19). Indeed the New Testament canon witnesses to divisions among Christians from the very start. The first letter attributed to the apostle John testifies to this when it says that "they went out from us, but they were not of us; for if they had been of us, they would have continued with us; but they went out, that it might be plain that they all are not of us" (1 Jn 2.19).

Orthodox Christians believe that the "genuine" who preserve and maintain the unity of the Church are those who are tested and approved. They are the "called and chosen and faithful" of the *Apocalypse* (Rev 18.14). They are the believing, baptized men and women who have "continued steadfastly in the apostle's doctrine, the communion, the breaking of the bread, and the prayers" (Acts 2.42). They are the fathers, mothers, martyrs, and saints of every age and generation—always few and always persecuted—who, with the faithful bishops in apostolic succession, believe the gospel (*evangelion*), receive the tradition (*paradosis*), and guard the deposit (*paratheke*) of the Church (2 Thess 2.15,3.6; 1 Tim 6.20).

Orthodox Christians believe that the Church's God-given unity—which is the unity still to be sought and found by the separated and divided churches—has been faithfully preserved only in the Orthodox churches of the Nicene and Chalcedonian faith and tradition that follow the canonized writings of the New Testament. Thus, Orthodox Christians consider the doctrine, order, and worship of all other Christian churches to be in some ways untrue, misleading, incomplete, or inaccurate.[5]

Confessing our sins and admitting our failures, both personal and corporate, Orthodox Christians participate in ecumenical activity in order to witness to these convictions and to overcome disagreements and divisions among the separated bodies. They do so while cooperating in all ways possible within the conditions of disagreement and division. They strive to identify and affirm what is good, true, right and beautiful, as they understand these divine realities, wherever they are found, within the churches and without. And they rejoice in the "vestiges of the Church" wherever genuine expressions of Christian teaching, sacramental life, sanctity, and service that the Lord inspires may be found, even in churches that the Orthodox cannot completely identify as Christ's holy Church. They try, according to their ability and strength, to cooperate with everyone without betraying "God's gospel" (Rom 1.1) and without compromising "the faith once for all delivered to the saints" (Jude 3): the faith received, guarded, elaborated, and transmitted, without error or change, in the Orthodox Church.

Progress toward Unity

Orthodox Christians involved in ecumenical activity believe that significant progress has been made in many ways. They are better able to distinguish between what is essential and nonessential in Christian life

---

[5]Dialogue between bishops and theologians of the Oriental and Eastern Orthodox churches has resulted in a united confession of faith concerning Christ's divinity and humanity, which may hopefully result in the restoration of unity between the two bodies. See footnote 6.

and teaching; to identify and affirm acceptable variations in teachings and practices; to assess and evaluate the "nontheological factors" affecting church unity; and to work with greater insight and clarity to overcome substantial disagreements and differences in the formal faith, order, and worship of the churches.

In doctrinal articulation, for example, an understanding has been reached between bishops and theologians of the anti-Chalcedonian Oriental churches and the pro-Chalcedonian Eastern churches about the unity of divinity and humanity in the person of God's incarnate Son and Word Jesus Christ. This official statement indicates that past christological disagreements and misunderstandings are settled and no theological obstacles remain to full eucharistic communion among these long-separated churches. What remains are the difficult tasks of coordinating liturgical worship, establishing appropriate organizational structures, healing painful memories, and convincing the members of these churches to accept interpretations of the original controversies in the light of the contemporary agreement. Such healing and reconciling efforts, which only come by God's grace and a willingness to refer all judgments about the past to God alone, allow the common understanding regarding the person of Christ to bring separated churches into full ecclesial unity.[6]

Progress has also been achieved between Eastern and Western churches concerning the understanding of the Holy Spirit's eternal procession from God the Father. Virtually all agree on the need to remove the *filioque* from the Nicene—Constantinopolitan Creed, or at least to explain it in a way acceptable to Orthodoxy without insisting on its

[6]"Communiqué of the Joint Commission of the Theological Dialogue between the Orthodox Church and the Oriental Orthodox Churches" (Abba Bishoy Monastery, Egypt: 20–24 June, 1988), *The Greek Orthodox Theological Review [GOTR]* 34.4 (Winter 1989) 393–397; Thomas Fitzgerald, "Toward the Reestablishment of Full Communion: The Orthodox–Orthodox Oriental Dialogue," *GOTR* 36.2 (Summer 1991) 169–182; "Joint-Commission of the Theological Dialogue between the Orthodox Church and the Oriental Orthodox Churches" (Orthodox Centre of the Ecumenical Patriarchate, Geneva, September 23–28, 1990), *GOTR* 36.2 (Summer 1991) 183–188; "Joint Commission of the Theological Dialogue between the Orthodox Church and the Oriental Orthodox Churches," (Orthodox Centre of the Ecumenical Patriarchate, Geneva, November 2–6, 1993). Negative reactions to the work of the joint commission have been expressed in the *Memorandum of the Sacred Community of the Holy Mountain* [Mt Athos] *concerning the dialogue between the Orthodox and the Anti-Chalcedonian Churches* (Karyai, 1995); and in *The Ethiopian Orthodox Church: Faith, Order of Worship, and Ecumenical Relations*, Chapter 27, 106–108.

inclusion in the creed.[7] But here too, there must be a healing of memories and a willingness to allow the churches to interpret the past in ways that permit them to retain their convictions, while honestly affirming and accepting a contemporary doctrinal agreement.

Progress has also been made in ecumenical circles in understanding the Orthodox Christian perspective of the Virgin Mary as *Theotokos* and in explaining her conception, birthgiving, dormition, and intercession in Orthodox Christian life and worship, in relation to both Roman Catholic and Protestant churches, the latter of which at one time not only excluded Christ's mother from their faith, worship, and spiritual life, but even from ecumenical discussion.[8]

Progress has also been made in recent decades in understanding the Church as a communal body in which all members have their proper place and ministry. Probably contemporary Orthodox thinkers have written more about the nature and task of the Church than any other subject. And, greater clarification has probably been achieved on this issue with and among Christians in the West, notwithstanding the unresolved differences and disagreements, than on any other. This seems to be particularly true in regard to the relationship between Scripture and tradition, authority and freedom, hierarchy and collegiality, governance and ministry, and the communion of local churches as each itself being, and all in communion comprising, Christ's one catholic Church.

Generally speaking also, the documents of the Second Vatican Council of the Roman Catholic Church, if not what has often be called the "spirit of Vatican II," are certainly more acceptable to Orthodoxy than the teachings of Vatican I, or the councils of Trent or Florence. The ecclesiastical order and liturgical rituals that accompany and actualize the statements of Vatican II are also in many ways more acceptable to

---

[7]The papal encyclical on the Holy Spirit *Dominum et Vivificantem* (1986) does not mention the *filioque*. The new *Catechism of the Catholic Faith* (1994) includes the *filioque* in the Creed and affirms and justifies it for the "Latin" and "Western tradition" (246–248), but does not mention it in the section "I believe in the Holy Spirit" (683–747). Cf. "The Greek and Latin Traditions regarding the Procession of the Holy Spirit," *L'Osservatore Romano* (September 20, 1995).

[8]Sadly, the brief explanations in *Catechism of the Catholic Church* continue to uphold the official dogmatic pronouncements on the "immaculate conception" and "assumption" of the Virgin Mary that Orthodox find unacceptable. More happily, Fr Sergius Bulgakov would not be ruled "out of order" today, as he was at the Faith and Order Meeting in Lausanne in 1927, for attempting to introduce the Virgin Mary into ecumenical discussion.

the Orthodox than the old Roman practices. This is particularly true regarding teachings and actions concerning the church and salvation, baptism and Eucharist, and the relation of the Roman Church to other Christian churches, particularly the Orthodox and Eastern rite churches united with Rome. Words of praise and hope are also in order in regard to the new *Catechism of the Catholic Church,* which presents and explains Christian doctrine on most issues in ways wholly acceptable to Orthodoxy.

Positive things also have resulted from the work of the Faith and Order Commission of the World Council of Churches such as the WCC Faith and Order documents *Baptism, Eucharist and Ministry*[9] and the *Explication of the Apostolic Faith as It Is confessed in the Nicene-Constantinopolitan Creed (381)*[10] (as well as the many different studies that went into the production of these documents and followed their publication). The changes that this work has effected in doctrinal teaching, liturgical worship, ecclesiastical polity, and spiritual life in many churches of Reformed traditions are to be commended.

These positive achievements, and many others, have somewhat tempered the "Orthodox agony" in the ecumenical movement lamented by Fr Alexander Schmemann forty years ago.[11] The discrepancies between "official" and "average" Orthodoxy and between the actual convictions of the majority of church members and the public face of the Orthodox Church certainly remain today. However, the Western, Protestant presuppositions that once reigned in the ecumenical movement are no longer in place, and ecumenical agencies such as the World Council of Churches are no longer virtually the only organs for ecumenical activity. This means that the Orthodox can now "participate" in a great variety of ecumenical activities, and not merely be "represented" in a few official organizations. It also means that they can exercise considerable impact on ecumenical activity. This does not mean, however, that the Orthodox will cease to be a minority in the

---

[9](Geneva, 1982). Cf. Baptism, Eucharist and Ministry 1982–1990, Report on the Process and Responses (Geneva, 1990), and *Orthodox Perspectives on BEM* (Brookline, 1985).

[10](Geneva, 1991).

[11]See Alexander Schmemann, "Orthodox Agony in the World Council," *Christianity Today* (January 20, 1958) 3–4; "Moment of Truth for Orthodoxy" in *Unity in Mid-Career: An Ecumenical Critique* (New York, 1963); and "The Ecumenical Agony" in *Church, World, Mission* (Crestwood, N.Y.: St Vladimir's Seminary Press, 1979).

ecumenical arena, often compelled to protest against majority decisions and actions. Still less does it mean that they will easily convince
others of the truths of Orthodoxy. But, it does mean that the Orthodox
need not participate in ecumenical work according to someone else's
rules, or simply be spectators who may, from time to time, make separate statements without much effect or attention. The real question,
however, is whether the Orthodox churches have the will, energy, and
resources to participate in ecumenical activity at all, given what is happening in their churches, in other churches that largely are uninter-
ested and disengaged from theological and ecclesiological decisions of
formal ecumenical bodies, and, of course, in the world as a whole.[12]

Old and New Obstacles

Whatever hope may exist in the quest for church unity, old obstacles
continue to stand in the way of achieving the unity we still seek for the
churches, and new obstacles have arisen to render the accomplishment
of full communion in faith, order, and worship among the churches
more unlikely than ever.

One fundamental and critical difficulty as regards church unity is
determining the formal authoritative position of a given church in matters of faith, order, and worship. Let me explain this dilemma.

More than seventy years ago at the First World Conference on Faith
and Order in Lausanne, and more than thirty-five years ago at the open-
ing of the Second Vatican Council in Rome, it was relatively easy to
determine the official beliefs and practices of various ecclesial com-
munions and confessional families. Their faith was clearly expressed
in their confessional statements, ecclesiastical structures, and corporate worship services, which were accepted and obeyed by the great
majority of their members. This is no longer the case.

[12]Cf. *The Ecumenical Movement, the Churches and the World Council of Churches*
George Lemopoulos, Ed.—an Orthodox contribution to the reflection process on "The
Common Understanding and Vision of the WCC" (Geneva and Bialystok, 1996). Also,
Todor Sabev, *The Orthodox Churches in the World Council of Churches* (Geneva and Bialystok, 1996). In January 2003, the "Final Report of the Special Commission on Orthodox
Participation in the WCC" was published in full in *The Ecumenical Review*, 55.1 (2003)
4–38. Published in the same volume were the "Action of the Central Committee in adopt-
ing the Final Report of the Special Commission on Orthodox Participation in the WCC"
(39–41) and "Frequently Asked Questions" about the report (42–48) and four articles critiquing the report's contents and significance (49–75).

Regarding the Roman Catholic Church, for example, the church's position is still clear on papal infallibility and the pope's universal episcopal authority and jurisdiction over all church members, including the other bishops. The bishop of Rome still claims and exercises special prerogatives in defining Christian doctrine and morals, and special rights over the bishops that he continues to appoint and whose legitimate episcopal authority still depends on their union with him and obedience to him, based on Rome's doctrines of "Petrine" privileges and powers.

The Orthodox Church still considers this Roman teaching and practice unacceptable to Christian faith and life for biblical, theological, and historical reasons (and not merely because of "Eastern" customs and traditions); and finds it incompatible with the gospel of God, the mystery of Christ, and the unity which God gives to his Church in his Son and Spirit. For the Orthodox—despite the need for ecclesial leadership, order, and witness on a worldwide level and the lamentable confusion that reigns among Christians in this area—the conviction holds that every bishop who receives the laying on of hands in apostolic faith, tradition, and historical succession is a successor of Peter and the apostles (none of whom was ever a bishop of a local church). Each such bishop is ordained to guarantee in his sacramental person and ministry the unity, identity, integrity, solidarity, and continuity of the faith and life of Christ's Church. And, each is called and consecrated to exercise fully the sacramental service of "rightly handling the word of truth," of "binding and loosing sins," and of "feeding the flock" of Jesus within the communion of baptized believers.[13]

In general, even with the many positive recent changes, the organization and operation of the Vatican continues to provide stumbling blocks on the path to Church unity from an Orthodox perspective. Obstructive issues for the Orthodox range from the manner in which Rome decides and enforces official church doctrine and discipline; to

---

[13] 2 Tim 2.15, Jn 20.22, and Jn 21.15–19, which in patristic commentaries is consistently referred to Peter's reinstatement as chief apostle after his three denials. Cf. *The Primacy of Peter. Essays in Ecclesiology in the Early Church*, John Meyendorff, Ed. (Crestwood, N.Y.: St Vladimir's Seminary Press, 1992). Also, John Erickson, "Collegiality and Primacy in Orthodox Ecclesiology," in *The Challenge of Our Past: Studies in Canon Law and Church History* (Crestwood, N.Y.: St Vladimir's Seminary Press, 1991); Thomas Hopko, "On Ecclesial Conciliarity," in *The Legacy of St Vladimir*, John Breck and John Meyendorff, Eds. (Crestwood, N.Y.: *St Vladimir's Seminary Press*, 1990).

the way bishops are assigned and saints are canonized; to teachings and practices on marriage, divorce, and celibacy; to Roman Catholic activities in regions where Orthodox leadership and church life have been gravely weakened by communist regimes.

A new thing in the Roman Church today which presents new difficulties in the quest for church unity from an Orthodox perspective is the fact that Roman Catholic bishops and priests, men and women religious, and laity sometimes confess convictions and condone practices contrary to the church's official teachings, including that of the papacy itself. Such dissension sometimes violates the ancient ecclesial principle that the Church's "rule of faith" (*regula fidei*) and its "law of believing" (*lex credendi*) and its "law of worship" (*lex orandi*) each affirm and establish the other in a unified witness to the one gospel. Such dissent makes it extremely difficult to determine what it means to be Roman Catholic today. It also permits one to think that the only requirement to be a Roman Catholic today is to participate sacramentally in a church united with Rome and to accept the authority of the pope in church life and teaching.

To determine the official stances of Anglican and Reformed traditions is also extremely difficult today because of the great variety of doctrines, orders, and forms of worship acceptable in these churches— whatever is formally voted upon by their respective administrative and judicial bodies. Long-standing difficulties concerning Scripture, tradition, doctrine, sacraments, and ministry, where significant progress seems to have been made at the end of the twentieth century, are now complicated by new teachings and practices. This is especially true regarding the authority and interpretation of the Bible, the uniqueness of Jesus; the relationship of Christians to non-Christians, and issues of ministry, sexuality, marriage, family life, and abortion.

Debates and disagreements on these issues have produced a host of new difficulties about the canon, authority, and interpretation of the Bible; the place of the ancient Church councils and canons; and the significance of church tradition. They affect the teachings and practices of the churches in regard to the naming of God, the baptismal formula, the use of the Lord's Prayer, and the understanding of the Trinity. They also produce insurmountable difficulties and divisions about the understanding of marriage and family, homosexuality, the ordination of women, and the requirements for ordination and participation in sacraments generally. They also affect the ways in which the churches understand and practice mission and evangelism, and explain and relate to the saving activity of God through Christ and the Holy Spirit outside the Christian Church.

Generally speaking, the greatest obstacle to church unity in the area of "order" is coming to a mutual understanding about the relationship of the priesthood of ordained ministers to the unique high priesthood of Jesus and to the priesthood of all who are baptized in Christ and sealed by his Spirit. As the responses to *Baptism, Eucharist and Ministry* demonstrated, the apparent agreements on baptism and Eucharist were revealed as illusory since disagreements still exist in the churches concerning the ministry.[14] These differences, including those concerning the churches' sacramental structures generally, seem less likely to be overcome due to the enormous changes in the teachings and practices of many churches in recent years.

What may happen, however, and indeed what seems to be happening, is that new alliances of Christians are occurring because of these controverted and disputed issues; divisions in established churches are paving a way for new agreements and unions among once-separated believers and ecclesial bodies. With God, and his "unsearchable judgments" and "inscrutable ways," all things are possible.

Orthodox Church Unity

Despite the many painful disagreements and divisions in the Orthodox Church due to the historical tragedies of recent centuries, Orthodox Christians are convinced that their churches have maintained a doctrinal, liturgical, and sacramental (if not historical and institutional) structure that can still be defended as fitting, proper, and adequate to the God-given unity of the Christian Church.

All Orthodox churches have their *relativists* who consider Orthodoxy as nothing but their peculiar tribal religion. They also all have their *zealots*, including those who, as in St Paul's time, do not always act "according to knowledge" and thereby replace God's righteousness with their own (Rom 10.2). They also all have *sectarians* who, along with some who identify themselves Orthodox while participating in

[14]Cf. Thomas Hopko, "Ministry and the Unity of the Church," *St Vladimir's Theological Quarterly*, 34.4 (1990).

noncanonical bodies, consider ecumenism as a heresy and even "pan-heresy." And, of course, they all have their hypocrites and sinners, alongside their martyrs and saints.

Theological, ecclesiological, liturgical, and canonical controversies abound in all Orthodox churches, as do disputes and divisions of personal, political, nationalistic, and ethnic nature. But with all this, and despite it all, the Orthodox churches continue to recognize each other as Christ's one holy Church by maintaining essential unity within and among themselves in doctrine, liturgy, spirituality, discipline, and the veneration of Orthodox saints. And, they all possess the same historical memory and identity.

Despite many doubts, hesitations, and temptations, virtually all Orthodox churches also continue to participate in ecumenical activity in one form or another. Their leaders and faithful members generally remain ready to affirm God's presence and action wherever it may be; to rejoice in all genuine elements of the Church's apostolic faith, order, worship, teaching, service, and sanctity wherever they be found; and to cooperate with everyone to the measure that they can. They also reject all formal and institutional deviations from sound Christian doctrine, right Christian worship, and proper Christian morality, while engaging in perpetual dialogue about these issues among themselves.

The Orthodox churches have managed to do this throughout decades, and in some cases even centuries, of the most relentless and cruel persecution and suffering. And, they continue to do so even when they cannot agree among themselves about such things as how their bishops should be elected and consecrated; how their primates should be ordered when they meet in council; how their churches outside traditionally Orthodox ecclesiastical territories should be established and governed; how the Ecumenical Patriarch of Constantinople should exercise his ministry of primacy in the modern world; or how they should participate in ecumenical activity.

Be all these things (and many others) as they may, the seeking and striving "that all may be one" in Christ's one holy Church remains an essential element of Orthodox Christian faith and life. To refuse to witness to Christ's unity with God, the unity of all creation in Christ, and the unity of Christ's holy Church, or to refuse in every way to affirm unity where it exists and to overcome division where it reigns, especially within and among Christian churches, must be considered by an

Orthodox Christian as nothing less than a betrayal of Christ and a blasphemy of the Holy Spirit. The Lord who prayed and gave his life "for the union of all"[15] and sent his Holy Spirit to "call all to unity' "[16] taught his disciples to do the same. After washing the feet of his apostles at the Last Supper, including the feet of the one who betrayed him, Jesus said to his disciples: "Truly, truly, I say to you, a servant is not greater than his master, nor is he who is sent greater than he who sent him. If you know these things, blessed are you if you do them" (Jn 13.16–17). Our Master says the same to us today.

---

[15]"For the peace from above, for the welfare of the holy churches of God, and for the union of all, let us pray to the Lord" (Byzantine Liturgy).

[16]"When the Most High came down and confused the tongues he divided the nations; but when He distributed the tongues of fire He called all to unity. Therefore, with one voice we glorify the all-holy Spirit" (Byzantine *Kontakion* of Pentecost).

Confessing the One Faith[1]

Christians zealous for the integrity of the Christian faith and the unity of Christians in the one Church of Christ may rejoice in the World Council of Churches (WCC) Faith and Order Paper No. 153 (1991) entitled *Confessing the One Faith: An Ecumenical Explication of the Apostolic Faith as It Is Confessed in the Nicene-Constantinopolitan Creed*. Should member churches of the WCC Faith and Order Commission (which includes the Roman Catholic Church) recognize this work as an acceptable foundation for further theological discussion within their respective churches and with others, Orthodox Christians may have hope that Christian ecumenism is moving toward its goal of the visible unity of Christians in the one Church of Christ, which Orthodox believe, of course, to be the Orthodox Church. Should the member churches have difficulty with this document, however, and substantially question its content, there would be virtually no hope for unity among the separated churches as desired by the Orthodox and envisioned by the pioneers of the ecumenical movement.

Confessing the One Faith may serve to bring together individuals and groups of believers from the divided churches into an agreement on a deeper, clearer, fuller explication of the apostolic faith, which may then lead them into unity in the one Church of Christ in a way not originally intended by the Faith and Order Commission. In a word, *Confessing the One Faith* may serve as a catalyst for the realignment of Christians beyond the bounds of the ecclesial bodies to which they now belong, through a process that, for many reasons, is already occurring beyond the bounds of formal and official ecumenical activity.

I offer my thoughts and comments on *Confessing the One Faith*, mindful of the warning given in its introduction:

[1]This paper was given at a conference in Moscow in September 2001 on the WCC Faith and Order Document, *Confessing the One Faith.*

... *Confessing the One Faith* is not intended to represent a consensus or even a convergence document that could as such provide a basis for the common recognition and confession of the apostolic faith as an essential element of visible unity among the churches. Rather, this study document should be seen as an instrument to help the churches to focus on and reflect together upon the apostolic faith. Such study and reflection should lead towards a fresh understanding of the apostolic faith and thus towards a common recognition and confession of this faith today. (*Confessing the One Faith*, Introduction, 19)

I take this paragraph to mean that we Orthodox Christians, together with other members of the Faith and Order Commission, are being asked to study and reflect on this document, by ourselves and with others, in order to test how well it succeeds in confessing the apostolic Christian faith as we understand, preach, and try to practice it in our churches today. If we find this document to be basically acceptable and usable, we should then be able to move on toward the goal of visible unity with those of like mind and similar sentiment. With this understanding, I will share three general reflections on the document and make twelve comments on specific issues.

The Christocentric Character of Christian Confession

My first concern about *Confessing the One Faith* is a concern that I have about Christian theology and teaching today generally, including most especially, among Orthodox theologians, pastors, and teachers. This is the concern that the centrality of Jesus Christ as witnessed in the canonical writings of the New Testament where the mystery of Christ is proclaimed and witnessed in the light of "the Law, the Psalms and the Prophets" of the Old Testament, is being displaced, and even lost, in the confused and stormy sea of historical and contemporary theological problems, methods, and concerns. The Nicene-Constantinopolitan Creed is, after all, a "symbol of faith" concerning the mystery of Christ. It is a statement elaborating the foundational and essential Christian confession that Jesus of Nazareth is Israel's messiah, the Son of the living God, the Lord and Savior of the universe. He is the one through whom all things came to be from God his Father. He is the messianic king who was crucified and glorified to receive authority to judge the living and the dead. He will come in glory at the end of the age to establish God's reign in the universe. Through him God ultimately and forever will be "all and in all."

The one God of the Nicene Creed, the Almighty (*pantokrator*), is the Father of Jesus Christ. Christ's Father is the one and only God, the creator of all things visible and invisible. The qualities and characteristics of this one God are taken from his revelation in Jesus. In a word, it is Christ alone who shows us who God is, what God does, and how God must be known and confessed. Christ shows us, as well, who the Holy Spirit is and how the Spirit is to be worshipped and glorified with the Father and the Son as the Lord and Giver of life who spoke through the prophets. The Church is Christ's Church: *one* with his unity with God, *holy* with his holiness, *catholic* with all the fullness of God that dwells in him bodily, and *apostolic* with the mission which he has received from the Father and entrusts to his disciples in the Spirit for the life of the world.

It seems to me that the fear of being charged with "Christomonism" or "Jesusism" or even "Christofascism"—or of not being sufficiently trinitarian or pneumatological, or of failing to be truly traditional or patristic or mystical or contemporary or even *orthodox*—has ironically caused many Christians, including many Orthodox, to a tragic confusion in the task, method, and order of confessing the Christian faith and elaborating Christian doctrine as was done by the church fathers, including those of Nicea and Constantinople. Obscuring the explicitly *christocentric* order of confessing Christian doctrine has created a mixture of ideas, assertions, and apologies, many, if not most (not to say virtually *all*) of which are found in *Confessing the One Faith* in a way quite typical of contemporary Christian writing, both ecumenical and confessional. In a word, things seem to be mixed together in a rather jumbled way without a clearly evangelical and apostolic *Christological* foundation, order, and elaboration throughout the document. This leads to confusion and difficulty in following arguments and drawing conclusions. Statements within the document are basically good and acceptable, but they are not expressed in the most clear and convincing way.

Confessing the One Faith confirms the urgent need to "return to the Fathers" and to "follow the Fathers," including those involved in the councils of Nicea and Constantinople, in their method and order of confessing the faith and elaborating Christian doctrine. Such a "return" and "following" of the Fathers will necessarily lead us beyond

them—directly to the Holy Scriptures and to the apostolic writings
that witness to God's gospel in Jesus, a process desperately needed
today in every area of Christian thought and activity.

The centrality of Christ is implicitly and pervasively present in *Confessing the One Faith*, as it is in Orthodox theology generally today.
But, this confession needs to be explicit and more focused. We should
confess, first and foremost, and throughout our confession of faith, that
it is indeed a confession about Jesus Christ, and his God, the Father
Almighty, and his Spirit who proceeds from the Father, and his Church
and his kingdom, which is that of God himself. This confession alone
will lead us today, as it led the early Church at Nicea and Constantinople, to a right and proper understanding, confession and explication of
the whole of the Christian faith in all of its aspects and elements.

Clarity about God

Greater care about the centrality of Christ in Christian confession will
inevitably lead to a desperately needed clarity about God in Christian
faith and theology, including Orthodox theology. Confusion about the
term "God" in *Confessing the One Faith* mirrors that of contemporary
theology, both ecumenical and confessional, including that of many
Orthodox. The different ways in which the word "God" is used in
Scripture and tradition must be more carefully and clearly stated, with
much greater consistency and discipline.

In the Bible and in traditional Christian liturgical worship, certainly
in the eucharistic Divine Liturgies of St John Chrysostom and St Basil
the Great, and most definitely in the Nicene-Constantinopolitan Creed,
the one true and living God, the only God there is, is the Father of Jesus
Christ. In this sense Jesus is not himself the one God. He is, as confessed
at Nicea, God's only Son who is "true God from true God." Neither is
the Holy Trinity, strictly speaking, the one God. There is no God *who*
is Father, Son, and Holy Spirit, as the document and confessional theology, including that of the Orthodox, so often declare. There are rather
three persons or hypostases in a very particular relationship of union
and communion. Two of the hypostases derive eternally from the first
who is the one God; and each of the hypostases is "God" in the sense of
being equally and identically divine—as we would say that Peter, Paul,
and Mary are each a "human being" in the sense of being equally and

identically human. Thus, as the Scriptures witness and the creed con-
fesses and the liturgy prays, there is the *one God and Father*; and the
Only-begotten Son Jesus Christ, begotten of the Father before all ages
and born of the Holy Spirit and the Virgin Mary as a real human being,
who was crucified and raised from the dead and is forever glorified "at
the Father's right hand"; and there is the Holy Spirit, who is not called
"God" in the creed, but is confessed to be co-worshipped and co-glori-
fied with the Father and the Son as truly "the Lord and Giver of life."[2]

In our confessions of faith we Christians must be very clear in dis-
tinguishing the four different ways of speaking about the one God, and
his Son Jesus Christ, and the Holy Spirit.

First, there are words for the *names* of the three divine hypostases:
Father, Son and Holy Spirit. Second, there are words for the divine properties and characteristics (*idiomata*) of God the Father and his Son and
Spirit, such as being, oneness, goodness, wisdom, power, love, et cetera,
that are always cataphatically confessed and apophatically qualified.
Third, there are words for the *activities* of the three divine hypostases
which always originate in the Father who is the principle (*arche*) and
cause (*aitia*) of all things, including his eternal Son and Spirit (pace
Confessing, p. 94); these activities are always accomplished by the
agency of the Son and the perfecting of the Spirit. And finally, there are
the *metaphors* for God the Father and his theanthropic Son and Holy
Spirit that are taken from every possible created thing: spiritual and
material, male and female, animal and vegetable and mineral, to which
the Holy Scriptures and writings of the saints bear witness.

The four ways of speaking about God—personal names, divine properties, divine activities, and metaphorical images—are not distinguished with sufficient clarity, care, and discipline in *Confessing the
One Faith.* Nor are they clearly and carefully distinguished in contemporary theological teaching, either Orthodox or non-Orthodox. To
speak of God as the Father with his Son and Holy Spirit is very different from speaking of God and Jesus Christ and the Holy Spirit as being
identically divine, eternal, good, true, wise, holy, strong, and so forth.
These ways of speaking about God and Christ and the Spirit are also
different from speaking about the three divine persons or hypostases in
terms such as creator, redeemer, sanctifier, savior, or sustainer, which

[2]Compare the eucharistic anaphoras of the divine liturgies of St John Chrysostom and
St Basil the Great with the Nicene symbol of faith.

are all terms for activities belonging in a certain, distinct order to all three of the persons of the Holy Trinity in communion. And it is yet another thing to speak about God and his Son and Spirit in images, metaphors, and similes, such as those referring to one or another of the divine hypostases as rock, light or wind; or as loving mother, roaring lion, or consuming fire. In my opinion *Confessing the One Faith* does not succeed in keeping these different usages clear and distinct. It speaks rather loosely and carelessly, creating unfortunate confusion rather than adequate confession. In this particular weakness the document mirrors much, not to say most, theological thinking and writing today, including that of the Orthodox.

Clarity about Church

A persistent difficulty in ecumenical discussion and documentation has not been successfully overcome in *Confessing the One Faith*: the need to distinguish carefully and accurately among the different meanings of the word "church." This is regrettable, since the production of this document afforded the perfect time and place for this significant achievement.

First of all, there is the theological meaning of Church, normally written with a capital "C," which is the object of faith confessed in the Nicene-Constantinopolitan symbol. This is the Church understood and confessed as the *una sancta catholica et apostolica*, Christ's Body and Bride, the pillar and bulwark of the truth, the fullness of him who fills all in all (cf. 1 Tim 3.15; Eph 1.23). This is the Church understood and confessed as the sacramental and mystical reality of human beings in communion with God through Christ in the Spirit, which is always found somewhere in a fitting and proper historical human form in a concrete human community where the gospel is rightly proclaimed, the mysteries of faith rightly celebrated, and the worship of God rightly ordered and accomplished.

The proper explication of this theological understanding of the Church—which is neither some sort of transcendent reality subsisting in various human communities in more or less successful ways, nor an invisible assembly of true Christian believers (perhaps even including righteous non-Christians) to be visibly manifested only at the end of the age in the Parousia of Christ—which is crucial to a confession of the one, apostolic Christian faith, is not found in the Faith and Order document No. 153. What is still found is confusion about how the Church is to be understood, explained, and believed in as confessed in the Nicene-Constantinopolitan Creed, and how this Church relates to the churches, written with a lowercase "c," as institutional and socio-logical entities—especially when we speak of the "church," a "church," or the "churches" as being sinful and separated, or as being organizations of oppression and injustice; or when we use the word "church" to describe a particular community, communion, or confes-sional family, for example, the Orthodox, Methodist, or Seventh-day Adventist "church."

The inability to achieve a clear and unambiguous distinction of these three uses of the term *church* in Christian theological state-ments, both ecumenical and confessional, may well be among the most significant weaknesses of Christian theology today. It may well also be a particular failing of the Orthodox, since so much has been written on this subject by eminent Orthodox thinkers, particularly in an ecumeni-cal context, in the last half century.[3] A Christian confession and expli-cation of the apostolic faith which would lead toward a "fresh understanding of the apostolic faith and thus toward a common recog-nition and confession of the faith today"—as *Confessing the One Faith* demands—must more adequately accomplish this task.

My reading of *Confessing the One Faith* has prompted me to iden-tify these three issues that I believe are in need of more accurate con-fession and explication of the apostolic faith than is found in the WCC Faith and Order document (and in contemporary theology generally). It also prompts me to raise issues not treated in the paper. I propose twelve such issues for further reflection and discussion.

1 The order (taxis) of Christian confession and doctrinal explication of the apostolic faith that emerges from a critical exegesis of the canon-ical New Testament Scriptures as they exegete and fulfill the Old Tes-tament Scriptures according to the evangelical "canon of faith" in Christ must be observed with greater discipline than is the case in *Con-fessing the One Faith*. It seems to me that though many, if not all, essen-tial things, are treated somewhere and somehow in the document in a

---

[3]A bibliography of writings in English by Orthodox authors about the doctrine of the Church is provided in T. Hopko, "On Ecclesial Conciliarity" in *The Legacy of St Vladimir* (Crestwood, N.Y.: SVS Press, 1990) 223–225.

substantially acceptable manner, the absence of a clear and disciplined Christocentric order of confession and explication makes it very difficult for its readers to work through the material in a way which allows them easily to grasp its meaning and significance. In a word, the document's format is not too "user-friendly." The issue of the order (*taxis*) of doctrinal confession and explanation must be carefully reconsidered.

2 The "one God, the Father Almighty" must be more clearly and unambiguously confessed and explained as the one God of Christian faith in relation to Jesus Christ as God's Son, as well as in relation to the Trinitarian Godhead (not the "Triune God," an expression so often used, yet not found in patristic writings or in Orthodox liturgical worship), and also in relation to the one God of Judaism and Islam.

3 The relationship between the one God and Father, the Son Jesus Christ, and the Holy Spirit, following scriptural teaching and interpreting classical synodical definitions, must also be more clearly confessed and explicated, especially in regard to the biblical basis of the Nicene formula. *Confessing the One Faith*, with much of contemporary theological writing, both ecumenical and Orthodox, is, in my opinion, in crucial need of such explanation in a more careful and consistent manner.

4 The identity of the eternal Son and Word of God with Mary's child must be confessed and explained with greater clarity. The present text seems at times to speak about some sort of relationship between God's Logos/Son and Jesus of Nazareth, as if God's Son and Word and Jesus Christ were not one and the same person. Expressions such as that "the eternal Son and Word of God was one with the human reality of Jesus" (Confessing, 109) or that "Jesus became man" (Confessing, 125) are examples of what I have in mind.

5 The virginity of Mary, not yet to speak of her ever-virginity, must be more directly confessed and explained in a foundational confession of the apostolic Christian faith than is done in *Confessing the One Faith*. Do Christians really believe that Jesus Christ, the Son of God, is eternally begotten of God the Father and born as a human being from the virgin Mary without human seed? In a word, does Jesus biologically have or have not a human father? If not, how is this to be explained, especially in regard to the confession of Christ's real, full, and true humanity? If so, how does this square with the apostolic faith as confessed in Scripture and in the Nicene Creed? Surely Orthodox theology

is in need of greater explication concerning the true and real humanity of Jesus Christ who is confessed as "one of the Holy Trinity" humanly born from the virgin.

6 Of absolute necessity today in regard to confessing the apostolic faith is an explication of the significance of gender and sexuality in the Christian view, beginning with the humanity and maleness of Jesus. Perhaps this issue, more than any other, reveals what people and churches really believe about God and Christ and the meaning of human being and life in the light of God's gospel in Jesus. Surely Orthodox theologians must work more diligently on this issue, given our traditional and present teachings and practices in regard to the relationship between men and women in the Church, with our convictions about marriage and family life, sexual behavior and procreation, and holiness and deification.

7 The confession of God, through Christ, being the "creator of all things, visible and invisible" was clearly intended originally to be a confession of belief in the existence of a "cosmos noetos," that is a world of invisible bodiless powers commonly called the angels. Do such beings actually exist? How are they to be understood in relation to God and creation? How are they to be understood in relation to biblical exegesis and to Christian liturgical worship? The spiritual world of the angels, with their relation to creation, is nowhere to be found in *Confessing the One Faith*.

8 To my knowledge the devil, and the demons generally, are yet to be mentioned in a Faith and Order document. The "demonic" may be mentioned, but not the devil or the demons. This is like mentioning the "divine," but not God, or the "spiritual," but not the Spirit. Is it not time to confront the issue of the existence, or non-existence, of the spiritual hosts who, according to Christian Scripture and worship, ceaselessly glorify God; the angelic messengers who interact with creatures; and the powers of darkness and hosts of demons under Satan's command whom, according to Scripture, Jesus casts out to prove his messiahship as God's Son, whose reason for appearing was "to destroy the works of the devil" (cf. 1 John 3.8)?

9 Given the work done by the Faith and Order Commission on the Holy Spirit, and most particularly on the specific issue of the procession of the Holy Spirit, one might have expected from *Confessing the One Faith* a clarion call to affirm the apostolic Christian faith as

holding that the Holy Spirit proceeds from the Father alone, with the *filioque* being at best an unfortunate addition to the creed done in good faith to affirm the full divinity of the Son of God. It is truly amazing to find the texts of the Nicene-Constantinopolitan Creed printed in the official edition of the document without the *filioque* in Greek and with the *filioque* in English, without explanation or comment. It seems that several Protestant churches that have dropped the *filioque* from the creed in their service books, and the Roman Catholic Church, which no longer demands the *filioque* from its united Eastern Churches and on solemn occasions of historical and ecumenical significance recites the creed without the *filioque* in deference not only to the Eastern tradition but also to the common tradition of apostolic Christianity, have gone further than the WCC Faith and Order Commission on this tragic issue, which is second in its church-dividing significance only to the Vatican dogma concerning the infallibility and direct jurisdiction of the Pope of Rome. Clarification about the *filioque* thus remains crucial to the task of confessing the one apostolic faith of Christians.

10 Surely the confession of faith in the one, holy, catholic and apostolic Church needs a clearer and deeper explication than is found in *Confessing the One Faith*. We must do better, as I mentioned above, to explain how human communities can legitimately claim the notes ascribed to the Church as an object of faith in the creedal confession of faith, and how the one Church of Christ may be truly identified with parishes, dioceses, national churches, and patriarchates, which, institutionally and sociologically speaking, are always to some measure divided, unholy, incomplete, and devoid of apostolic fervor and action. Much excellent material exists on this subject by Orthodox and non-Orthodox theologians, as well as in many ecumenical statements over the past half century. Sadly, this material has not been used to much advantage in *Confessing the One Faith*.

11 As the Faith and Order Paper No. 111 (1982) on *Baptism, Eucharist and Ministry* so clearly demonstrated, together with the massive, wholly unexpected response to it from thousands of churches, organizations, conferences, institutes, schools, pastoral groups, and individuals, the issue of ministry and authority in the Church is of greatest significance in demonstrating how churches and individual believers understand and apply the apostolic Christian faith in their actual lives. A document intending to be a helpful instrument for

focusing and reflecting on the apostolic faith must deal with these issues more deeply and carefully than does *Confessing the One Faith*. Surely the issues of church structure and order and authority, with an understanding of the ministries of bishops, presbyters, deacons, and lay people, are essential to a discussion of the apostolic faith of Christians. So too, especially today, is a forthright discussion of the papacy in the Roman Catholic Church, as well as the issue of women (and more recently, gay men and lesbians) in Christian life and service.

12 And finally, the issue of salvation is in need of a more careful and developed treatment than is found in our document. In addition to a more adequate explication of the significance of the "one baptism for the remission of sins," with its relation to the gift of the Holy Spirit to the newly baptized, two aspects of this issue are of particular importance: the salvation of "all Israel" and the salvation of all creatures. What is the place of the Jews in God's design of salvation in Christ? Shall all Jewish people, and all people generally, be saved in God's kingdom? Does everlasting gehenna exist for anyone? Are some of God's creatures everlastingly shut out of God's kingdom? If so, what does this say about God as Love and Christ as Savior? These issues must be forthrightly treated today, ecumenically and within the various churches, surely within the Orthodox Church, with greater care and depth than is currently the case.

These are my reflections and comments on *Confessing the One Faith*. They have more to do with the order, carefulness, and contents of the document than with its content, which, as far as it goes, is in my view substantially acceptable. As I already stated, I believe that the work is encouraging for Orthodox Christians as "an instrument to help the churches to focus on and reflect together upon the apostolic faith." I hope that my thoughts on the document prove helpful toward this end as well.

Orthodoxy and Ecumenism[1]

N
ew and strong voices are heard in world Orthodoxy in recent years condemning the participation of the Orthodox churches in ecumenism. These voices belong mostly to people who have never, or hardly ever, participated in ecumenical work. In former communist countries whose Orthodox populations for many reasons are strongly anti-Roman Catholic, anti-Protestant and anti-Western generally, the denouncers of Orthodox participation in ecumenism are now also found especially among those who criticize their ecclesiastical leaders from Marxist times when their churches began to participate in ecumenical organizations and projects. The entrance of persecuted Orthodox churches into ecumenical activity during the communist period was part of a strategy of survival that is now severely criticized in these churches.

Rejection of ecumenism in former communist regions today, in addition to the historical anti-Westernism, is also caused by the incursion of proselytizing "missionaries," Christian and non-Christian, into these now free and democratic countries. Most of the proselytizers, ironically, are from churches, sects and religions that were never involved in ecumenism. In some Old World countries, such as Bulgaria, Georgia, and Israel, opposition to ecumenism, with the decision to withdraw from the World Council of Churches (WCC) and other ecumenical organizations, has been almost exclusively motivated by internal political reasons.

In North America and Western Europe the strongest denunciations of ecumenism and Orthodox participation in ecumenical work seem to come from converts to Orthodoxy.[2] The conservative converts were usually anti-ecumenical before joining the Orthodox Church. Converts from

---

[1]This is a summary of talks and lectures on Orthodoxy and ecumenism given in various settings in recent years.

[2]Some of the strongest anti-ecumenical voices in Eastern European Orthodox churches are recent converts to Orthodoxy. My impression is that converts generally tend to be hypercritical of the non-Orthodox and hardly critical of Orthodoxy in any way

liberal churches generally come to Orthodoxy because of the apostasy from basic Christian teachings and practices by their church leaders.

Condemnation of Orthodox participation in ecumenical activity, both in America and abroad, also comes from some Orthodox monastics and their disciples who identify as their mission the preservation of "pure" and "undefiled" Orthodoxy in the face of possible stain and blemish from the heterodox. These monastic zealots, with their spiritual children, are often not only anti-ecumenical, they are also anti-Oriental Orthodox, anti-Roman Catholic and anti-Protestant generally. They see virtually nothing but error, danger, and harm coming from these people and their heterodox churches, which they hardly recognize as Christian. They generally apply to non-Orthodox Christians what the holy fathers and church canons said in reference to heretics, (which at that time usually meant bishops in Orthodox churches who claimed to be orthodox but were teaching false doctrines). They insist that Roman Catholics and Protestants, and also the Oriental Orthodox, must simply recant their errors, repent of their sins, and join the Eastern Orthodox Church. They see no possibility for these Christian communities to make common confessions of faith with the Orthodox, with provision for interpretations of their histories, adjustments in their liturgies, and changes in their ecclesial structures—all of which would heal disagreements, overcome divisions, and allow for, and even require, reconciliation and reunion.

Denunciations of ecumenism also come from leaders of the Russian Orthodox Church Outside Russia (ROCOR) and their supporters, those both within ROCOR and without. They also come from "old calendar" and "traditionalist Orthodox" intellectuals, the more vocal of whom are also mostly converts to Orthodoxy. Sometimes the anti-ecumenical position of these groups is but one element in a wider and deeper opposition to the teachings and practices of other Orthodox churches (or "jurisdictions") for national, cultural, historical, ideological, political, and sometimes even personal reasons.

What is novel about the recent denunciations of ecumenism, and Orthodox participation in it, besides the fact that they are made in

because of their gratitude in finding the Orthodox Church. Those raised in Orthodoxy, on the other hand, with no less gratitude for being Orthodox than converts, are often more ready and able to acknowledge and criticize Orthodoxy's institutional weaknesses and failures, even feeling a certain duty to do so, while affirming, rejoicing in, and at times even being envious of, the good things of God that exist outside the Orthodox Church.

radically new conditions for Orthodoxy, Christianity generally, and humankind as whole, is that they consider Orthodox involvement in ecumenical work as a betrayal of Orthodoxy itself. This position is for the most part based on the false premise that participation in ecumenism requires the Orthodox to embrace some sort of "branch theory" ecclesiology that denies that the Orthodox Church is alone the one, holy, catholic and apostolic Church of Christ. It is also based on the fear, especially in Eastern Europe, that if ecumenism succeeds the Orthodox Church will be forced to give up its beautiful and beloved liturgical practices and traditions.[3]

Opponents of Orthodox ecumenical work are often also mistakenly convinced that the goal of ecumenical organizations and activities is to create an all-inclusive "super church" in which practically any doctrines and practices are accepted, however outrageously unchristian.[4] They see Orthodoxy being absorbed into this new "ecumenical church of the future" now being prepared by "ecumenism." They also wrongly believe that the Orthodox who participate in ecumenical work receive communion in non-Orthodox services and give Orthodox sacraments to the heterodox, particularly at ecumenical meetings and events. And, they accuse those who participate in ecumenism in any way as being, at best, fools and opportunists, and, at worst, heretics and apostates.

The sharpest and least informed attack on Orthodox participation in ecumenical work is that ecumenism in any form or from any perspective is the "heresy of heresies." It is "the pan-heresy" that includes every deviation from Orthodox Christianity ever taught and practiced by heterodox Christians.

[3]As an astonishing example, a priest from an Orthodox Church in a formerly communist country who never attended an ecumenical meeting but was violently opposed to ecumenism went to a Protestant church in the West that was helping his church financially; he received communion there at a Lord's Supper service. He was surprised when questioned about this, seeing nothing wrong or illogical in his behavior. "We have ours," he said, "and they have theirs. I participated in their symbolic service out of friendship. I saw no reason to offend them. But I will never change or surrender our Orthodox faith." A reverse story of similar spirit and content concerns a Russian Orthodox woman in America who was a passionate defender of the old calendar, Slavonic in the Liturgy, and no changes in church services. Yet, she strongly insisted that her non-Orthodox grandsons be robed with the altar boys and receive Holy Communion when they came to her church once a year on "Old-style" Christmas.

[4]Some liberal Protestants may hold this view, but the great majority of churches and people involved in ecumenical work do not. Such a view, for example, has been strongly and consistently condemned in official statements of the WCC.

Innovations in Orthodoxy

The condemnation of ecumenism, and its identification as apostasy and heresy, is something new in the Orthodox Church. It is an innovation that has entered Orthodoxy in recent decades, together with other innovations of similar nature.

An example of a similar innovation in Orthodoxy is the teaching that no churchly character or sacramental grace of any kind exists in non-Orthodox churches. Another more extreme variant is that non-Orthodox Christians are not Christians at all, and their churches are not in any sense churches; thus, heterodox believers may be called "Christians," and their communities called "churches," only sociologically. Or it may be that under certain conditions, always for purely practical reasons, by using a strange new (and unacceptable) understanding of *oikonomia*, the Orthodox are thought to have the right and power to supply spiritual or sacramental realities to non-Orthodox churches which these bodies in fact do have in any way. Those holding these new views also generally make no distinction between the pastoral treatment of heresiarchs and their often quite innocent victims, many of whom find themselves in heretical churches through no choice of their own, sometimes after literally hundreds of years of their churches' separation from Orthodoxy.

Other new teachings and practices, virtually unknown in Orthodoxy until recent centuries, abound. One modern innovation is that all converts to Orthodoxy, including those from all heterodox Christian churches without exception, are to be baptized upon entering the Orthodox Church. Another is that converts themselves can decide whether or not they want to be baptized upon entering the Orthodox Church. Another is that members of the Orthodox Church who were not baptized upon joining the Church may do so after years, even decades, of receiving the Holy Eucharist in the Orthodox Church—including priests who have been serving the sacraments in Orthodox churches. Another is that Orthodox Christians not baptized by complete immersion, even if their baptisms were in an Orthodox church, should go through such a baptism, even, once again, if they are Orthodox priests.

Another conviction found in recent years among some members of the Orthodox Church is that all teachings, practices, and traditions found in Orthodox churches belong to the Church's very being and cannot be categorized, distinguished, or debated as to their essential or nonessential character. Those holding this view find it impossible to consider that some teachings, practices, and traditions found currently in Orthodox churches are not Orthodox, but have entered the churches under outside influences. Another new conviction is that no liturgical renewal of any kind is necessary, or even possible, in the Orthodox Church. Yet another is that all of the teachings of all canonized Church fathers and saints are right and true in every respect, exist in total harmony with each other, and are even a form of "divine revelation."

These new practices necessitate that a person's fidelity to God, Christ, the Holy Spirit, and the Church be measured in exact proportion to their acceptance without question or exception of all teachings and practices found in Orthodox churches, and their simultaneous denial of any existence of God, Christ, the Holy Spirit, and the Church outside of Orthodoxy. To question any teaching or practice in the Orthodox Church, or to affirm and recognize any teaching or practice outside it, renders one subject to the charge of being proud, arrogant, ignorant, and desirous of heterodox approval and acceptance. In fact, it renders one unfaithful to Orthodoxy.

All these new teachings, which to greater or lesser degrees accompany the condemnation of Orthodox participation in ecumenism, are relatively recent in the Orthodox Church. They are unknown in the Bible and in Orthodox Church history until recent centuries (the eighteenth and nineteenth centuries) when virtually all Christian churches were condemning all others in the most polemical manner, often within violent conditions of military occupation and religious persecution and oppression. They are not found among Orthodox Church fathers and saints until these recent centuries, including those who urgently warned their disciples to avoid the company of immoral persons, unbelievers, and heretics, and to stay away from their gatherings, while they themselves went among them to try to win them to God.

Traditional Criticisms of Ecumenism

However new the wholesale condemnation of Orthodox participation in ecumenism is in recent times, critiques of Orthodox participation in ecumenical work by Orthodox ecumenists are not new at all. They are, in fact, so constant and consistent since the beginning of Orthodox involvement in ecumenism, they could be considered a customary and essential aspect of the work. Such criticisms of ecumenism persist among Orthodox involved in ecumenical activity through today.

The criticisms of ecumenism from those who have dealt first-hand with ecumenism from their personal experiences are many. These critics have evaluated official reports and actions at ecumenical gatherings, and have largely remained indifferent to statements and actions not part of the official proceedings—regrettably these latter, more sensational activities are often reported by the media. They also criticize the spirit, organization, and conduct of ecumenical meetings; the manner and quality of participants; and the contents of the carefully crafted documents produced by the assemblies and conferences. They also interpret and scrutinize the decisions and actions taken by ecumenical bodies, together with their subsequent interpretations and applications.

The established critics of Orthodox participation in ecumenical organizations and activities, however, never criticized or condemned ecumenism as such, nor did they consider ecumenism to be a heresy. Nor did they think that Orthodox involvement in ecumenism was an act of apostasy from Orthodoxy. On the contrary, they defended proper and competent Orthodox participation in ecumenical work, and criticized what they judged as improper and incompetent. They defended what they believed to be a right understanding of ecumenism. Further, they criticized statements and actions of Orthodox participants at ecumenical events that they considered to be ambiguous, misleading, irresponsible, self-serving, or simply mistaken and sinful. They also censured documents, statements, decisions, and actions of ecumenical organizations, assemblies, and conferences, as well as those of professional ecumenical leaders, for the same reasons.

Orthodox participants at ecumenical gatherings also have assessed critically the common worship at ecumenical meetings—particularly when these services were unacceptable to Orthodoxy. On some occasions Orthodox participants have absented themselves from these services, or have protested against them after the fact, when they were caught unaware of the structure and content of the service. When making such criticisms, however, Orthodox participants never considered that common worship with non-Orthodox Christians in ecumenical settings, when properly done, with recognition of the divisions among the churches and petitions for God's assistance and guidance, was sinful or wrong. They certainly did not consider such prayer to violate the Orthodox Church's canonical rules against "praying with heretics." Indeed the Orthodox themselves recognized the need for common prayer, Scripture study, and silent meditation in ecumenical settings, so that God would bless the work according to his divine word and will. Further, some Orthodox ecumenists also criticized the way that the Orthodox themselves organized and participated in (or did not organize or participate in) their own Orthodox liturgical services at ecumenical gatherings.

Finally, many Orthodox participants and advocates of ecumenism, though favoring ecumenism in theory, have at times called for withdrawal from formal ecumenical organizations, but not from ecumenical activities generally, for practical reasons. The most frequent pragmatic argument against Orthodox participation in ecumenism, especially membership in official ecumenical organizations and conferences, always has been the lack of serious interest, resources, planning, and collaboration in ecumenical work on the part of the Orthodox churches themselves. "Either let's do it right and responsibly," participants and churches often argued, "or let's not do it at all. It is too shameful and embarrassing!"

More importantly, Orthodox ecumenists have always believed that ecumenism, rightly understood and practiced, is an essential element in the life and work of the Orthodox Church. It is a sacrificial ministry required of Orthodox Christians in the present conditions of the world and an act of fidelity to Christ in obedience to God for the good of others. It is a God-given opportunity, inspired by the Holy Spirit, for Orthodox Christians and churches to serve and ask nothing in return but that God's will would be done by those who invoke Christ's holy name.

Origins of Ecumenism

Although there are examples of ecumenical activity in the nineteenth century, the birth of ecumenism as we now know it began in the first decades of the twentieth century.[5] Western Christians had been divided into countless warring churches and sectarian groups for nearly four hundred years. Eastern Christians, internally divided since the fourth

[5]Cf. G. Florovsky, "Orthodox Ecumenism in the Nineteenth Century," *St Vladimir's Theological Quarterly*, 4.3–4 (1956): 2–53.

century, also had been separated from Western Christians for nearly nine hundred years. All of these Christians passionately disagreed about Christian doctrine, worship, mission, and service in fiercely divided churches; they all became involved in two bloody world wars, fought mostly in their own countries, mostly against each other. Christians had been fighting among themselves militarily, politically, culturally, economically, and religiously for centuries, and many Christian leaders, mostly Protestant and some Orthodox (and even some Roman Catholic, though not yet with the endorsement of the Vatican), began to seek a solution to these conflicts and divisions. Thus, Christian ecumenism was born from the mutilated and murdered bodies of millions of men, women, and children, most of whom were Christians.

The tasks and goals of ecumenism from the beginning were simple and clear.

Representatives of the divided Christian churches had to meet peacefully in formally organized ways. They had to discuss their theological differences in a free and respectful manner; to clearly pinpoint the causes of their theological and ecclesial divisions, and to work, to the measure possible, to overcome them. This process came to be called the work of faith and order. They had also to organize their churches' evangelical and missionary activities in ways that would minimize confusion and harm to those to whom they ministered. And, they had to mutually support the poor, needy, sick, suffering, homeless, and dispossessed—especially victims of natural disasters, wars and revolutions—which they could do, despite theological differences and ecclesiastical divisions.[6]

Although, ecumenism was originally a Protestant and Anglican creation, Orthodox representatives, if not genuine "participants" (to employ Fr Alexander Schmemann's famous distinction), were present from its inception.[7] By 1961, Orthodox churches under communist domination had joined the World Council of Churches (WCC), which had been founded in 1948; thus, all Orthodox churches were by then

[6]Countless Orthodox Christians in exile from their homelands because of communist persecution were helped by ecumenical efforts: settling Orthodox refugees; providing places for Orthodox worship; and supporting Orthodox clergymen and assisting Orthodox educational and philanthropic activities. It is impossible to imagine what would have happened to these millions of Orthodox Christians without the aid and assistance of non-Orthodox Christians.

[7]Cf. "The Unity We Still Seek" in this present volume.

members. The Eastern European Orthodox entered the WCC, it must be emphatically noted, only on condition that the organization's charter restricted membership to Christian churches proclaiming the lordship of Jesus Christ whose members were baptized in water in the name of the Holy Trinity.

Challenges of Ecumenism

Though the tasks and goals of ecumenism were simple and clear, their execution was not—given the number and variety of churches, the magnitude of the issues, and the complexity of the problems. Because of its European and American Protestant and Anglican origins, ecumenism was particularly difficult, complex, and troubling for Orthodox churches, since it cast issues in non-Orthodox categories from the outset. It was rendered even more difficult and complex for the Orthodox because of the Orthodox themselves, especially after 1961, when all Orthodox churches began to participate.

Additionally, the Orthodox were ill-prepared for ecumenical work; they had difficulties in relating to each other; they didn't know each other's languages; their churches were mostly poor and persecuted; their churches competed with each other; each had its own political agenda, both ecclesiastical and secular, and most were from Marxist dominated regions. Ecumenical gatherings were virtually the only place where Orthodox Christians from different churches and countries were free to meet and speak. Only a few people in each church were prepared to participate competently in ecumenical work, even in the most minimal and tentative ways. Some came to make careers in ecumenism, enjoying the personal advantages that ecumenical activity afforded, like income, travel, and involvement with interesting and prestigious people. In a word, the ecumenical scene, though not without its positive and pleasant aspects, was for the Orthodox always difficult, complex, confusing, and painful. It was fraught with temptations and troubles on the right hand and on the left. Everyone suffered to some extent; the people who were called to participate, those who wanted to, but were not selected; and the churches' leaders and members who for the most part did not really understand what was going on.

Problems in ecumenism multiplied as the ecumenical movement grew and developed. Ecumenical organizations, such as the WCC and the National Council of Churches of Christ (NCCC) in America became larger, and more complex and bureaucratic. The acquisition and use of money and resources became controversial issues. People of particular ideologies took power and used ecumenical agencies to advance their political and social agendas. The perennial human problems of power, position, possessions, prestige, pleasure, profit, and personal rivalries appeared and proliferated. Again, it could hardly be otherwise. This led not only to struggles of all sorts, but also caused many to question the methods and operations of ecumenical organizations and agencies, as well as their capacity to accomplish the tasks and goals for which they were originally created and intended.

In addition to personal, bureaucratic, and organizational issues, the challenges of changing theological and ethical positions and practices in the churches made ecumenism more trying and troubling. In Lima in 1981, for example, when the famous *Baptism, Eucharist and Ministry* (BEM) document was completed and accepted by the WCC Faith and Order Commission (which by then had Roman Catholics as official members), Protopresbyter Vitaly Borovoi of the Russian Orthodox Church, a longtime and longsuffering Orthodox ecumenical worker, made a prophetic statement. Though BEM did not deal with the issue of the ordination of women, Fr Vitaly solemnly warned that the ordination of women as priests and bishops in certain churches would lead to changes in teaching and practice that would render them unrecognizable as Christian bodies. He saw that everything from the naming of God, to family life and marriage, to issues of sexual behavior, to ways of worship and everyday living would be radically recast. In a word, he foresaw the painful problems that confront Orthodox Christians who participate in the ecumenical movement today.

Harmful Effects of Ecumenism

Many critics have argued that ecumenism has greatly harmed the Orthodox churches.[8] They argue that instead of witnessing to the truth

[8]For example see Fr John Reeves, "The Price of Ecumenism. How Ecumenism Has Hurt the Orthodox Church," *The Christian Activist*, 9 Fall/Winter (1996): 36–42. My view is that the "horrors" in contemporary Christianity that Fr John enumerates and decries are not, as he claims, the result of ecumenism. They derive from other developments in Western, especially American, Christianity that have themselves largely produced the wrong understanding of ecumenism that not only Orthodox Christians, but many Protestants

of the gospel and the Orthodox faith, the Orthodox themselves, through their representation and participation, have succumbed to the spirit of relativism, modernism, and apostasy. They also argue that heresy is intrinsic to ecumenism.

It is true that many members of the Orthodox Church, particularly in Western Europe, North America, and Australia, have succumbed to religious relativism, individualism, subjectivism, and indifference. Many understand toleration to mean that no one is right or wrong, that all religions and churches are equally good or bad, that none can claim ultimate and definitive truth. It is also true that members of Orthodox churches in the United States have succumbed to what is called "American civil religion" in which their ultimate allegiance is to "the American way of life." Participating nominally in church life, they display greater obedience and honor to American laws, values, holidays, shrines, political leaders, and national traditions. But all this has nothing to do with ecumenism as originally conceived and properly enacted. It has, however, everything to do with ecumenism as understood and practiced in its peculiarly American setting. And, it has everything to do with modern and post-modern thinking, particularly of the secularized Northern and Western parts of the globe, which has as often been censured in ecumenical settings by Christians of all churches as it has been endorsed by many ecumenical leaders educated in these parts of the world.

When speaking of harmful effects, the stern reminder that St John Chrysostom sent to St Olympia from his place of exile comes to mind. He wrote to his sad, angry, and despairing co-worker that "no one can harm him who does not harm himself." He worked through the entire Bible to make his point. God's people always suffer, he reminded his beloved friend. But unless they harm themselves, nothing can harm them. They certainly cannot be harmed by going among sinners and evildoers (not to speak of good-willed victims of Christian divisions) to do the Lord's work with the Holy Spirit working with them.

---

and Roman Catholics, have consistently criticized and rejected. At the end of his article Fr John calls for a "new ecumenism" among "conservative" Christians in which he envisions strong Orthodox participation. This should prove that he is not against ecumenism as such, but against the wrong thinking and bad behavior of many of those involved in the ecumenical activity that he describes and denounces. The title of his essay is therefore misleading.

Meeting and working with those who claim to be Christians in order
to witness to the gospel of Christ and "the faith once for all delivered
to the saints" (Jude 3) is an essential work of Orthodox Christians. No
one can be harmed in doing this work, unless they harm themselves.
Harm comes to those who refuse to serve God and to suffer in and for
Christ, whatever the situation and setting. Harm especially comes to
those who refuse to go where Christ's holy name is invoked, whether
for evil or for good, in order to witness to goodness and truth. And harm
surely comes to those who refuse so to serve Christ and their neighbors
because of self-righteousness, cowardice, arrogance, pride, fear, envy,
and judgment of others. And, harm comes most of all to the leaders of
the churches who have been given the grace, authority, and duty to govern Christ's flock, to feed and protect his sheep, and to bring back into
the fold those who have strayed, often through no fault of their own.

The original tasks and goals of ecumenism have not changed. They
have only become more complex, troubling, and painful. For the Orthodox to withdraw from ecumenical activity now, after all their sufferings and achievements, modest though they be, like the recent
reforming of WCC structures and methods of operation, would be a
spectacular victory for the devil and his co-workers. It would be a capitulation of magnificent proportions to evil.[9]

The Lord Jesus Christ prayed to his Father for his disciples before his
Passion. He prayed not only that "they may be one" as he and the
Father are one (by far the most quoted biblical passage in ecumenical
speeches and documents), but also that the Father should not take his
faithful followers out of the world, but that he should "keep them from
the evil one" (Jn 17.11,15). As long as Christ's disciples are in the world,
they must use everything in their power, including ecumenical agencies and activities, to glorify God and to serve their fellow creatures,
especially fellow Christians. They must use everything that they can,
however modest and mean and ambiguous and painful, to work with
Christ, "the Son of God [who] appeared," as St John has written, "to
destroy the works of the devil" (1 Jn 3.8).

[9]Cf. *The Ecumenical Review*, 51.4 (1999), which is almost entirely dedicated to Orthodox participation in the ecumenical movement, and *The Ecumenical Review*, 55.1 (2003),
which contains the "Final Report of the Special Commission on Orthodox Participation
in the WCC," along with the WCC Central Committee's official action on this report, several pages of questions and answers about it, and four articles critiquing its contents and
significance.

Ecumenism, now more than ever, needs the humble and humiliated witness of the Orthodox churches. It requires the patient and persistent testimony of those who are ready to make fools of themselves wherever Christ's name is invoked so that it be not betrayed or blasphemed, but obeyed and glorified. Perhaps the Orthodox can do nothing in contemporary ecumenism but be there like confessors, martyrs, and fools for Christ. But be there they must, for their own edification and salvation, and for that of their churches. The Lord will see that they are not harmed in doing his will.

Fruits of Ecumenism

Questions have also been raised about the fruits of ecumenism for the Orthodox churches, with contemporary critics claiming that none at all can be found. After more than a half-century of ecumenical participation, they argue, the Orthodox churches have received only humiliation and harm. The influence of Orthodoxy on the non-Orthodox has been negligible, they say; the converts to Orthodoxy have been few. The developments in the Christian churches have been incomparably more negative than positive in almost every conceivable way. The Christian churches are now further apart than ever. Looking more deeply into the issue, however, and from a more biblical and traditional Christian perspective, may lead to a different conclusion.

First of all, the most precious fruit of ecumenism for the Orthodox in the light of Christ's gospel is that participation in ecumenical work provides the Orthodox with an unique opportunity to witness to Christ in territory largely held by the devil who constantly works to deceive, divide, and destroy those who seek God and desire to do his will.

Ecumenical work, especially in the present time, affords magnificent opportunities for Orthodox Christians to love their enemies, to do good to those who hate them, to bless those who curse them, and to pray for those who abuse them. It provides countless occasions for them to speak with those who may not at all want to speak with them. It definitely gives chances not to resist evildoers, but to turn the other cheek to those who strike and attack by words and deeds. And it certainly produces plenty of possibilities to offer many good things to others, asking nothing in return for oneself or one's church. Indeed, should not the proper question for Orthodox Christians be what they can *give* to others through their participation in ecumenical work, rather than what they can *receive*? Ecumenical gatherings also continue to provide opportunities for Orthodox Christians to meet each other and to work together in ways that they never could do, or would do, without these forums.

Ecumenism also provides opportunities for Orthodox to meet good people who are not in their Orthodox churches. The Orthodox can come to know that Protestants and Catholics and members of the Oriental Orthodox churches, for all the errors and mistakes of their respective churches, can be real disciples of Jesus Christ. They can see this, for example, in their genuine praising of Christ, their devoted Christian scholarship, their acts of mercy for the poor, their care for the needy, and their service to suffering people (including Orthodox people) in Christ's name. They can see it as well in their suffering, sometimes unto death as martyrs, for the Christian faith and the glory of God.

Participants at ecumenical encounters and events also learn that countless misunderstandings exist among Christians about one another and their respective churches—misinformation or plainly untrue information abounds. Countless Christians in non-Orthodox churches, including those active in ecumenical work even at very high levels, know almost nothing about Orthodoxy, and what they do know is often inaccurate. Certainly many non-Orthodox Christians are unhappy in their own churches, deeply disagreeing with their leaders who have departed from fundamental teachings of the Christian faith; they welcome the opportunity to learn about the Orthodox faith.

The Ecumenical movement also has forced Orthodox Christians to formulate and confess their convictions. Indeed some of the most valuable books and articles on Orthodoxy, especially about the nature of the Church, the interpretation of the Bible, the meaning of liturgical worship, and the practice of spiritual struggle were written for ecumenical conferences and meetings. And, countless changes in the ways of understanding, confessing, worshipping, and living the Christian faith have occurred in non-Orthodox churches because of the witness of the Orthodox. The decisions of Vatican II are an example of this, as are changes in theology, worship, and spiritual life in Protestant churches. Good things in religious life happen quietly and slowly with no coverage in the media, and the great majority of Christians in the world, even in Western Europe and America, still, for the most part, adhere to basic biblical teachings.[10]

Ecumenism also has forced the Orthodox to be honest about themselves and their churches. The production of ecumenical statements, for example the WCC's Faith and Order document on *Baptism, Eucharist and Ministry* and the responses to it by the churches, clearly show that the Orthodox often do not themselves practice what they preach and teach. Orthodox ecumenical rhetoric, the record reveals, is often quite far from Orthodox ecclesial reality.

We Orthodox all too often say one thing at ecumenical meetings, and do something else in our own churchly actions. An example of this is the discrepancy between Orthodox "ecumenical witness" regarding liturgical and sacramental worship and actual Orthodox practice. Another example is the Orthodox ecclesiology regarding church structures and governance presented at ecumenical meetings, and how Orthodox hierarchs, including heads of autocephalous churches and ecclesiastical jurisdictions, actually relate to each other and to the clergy and laity in their churches. If the only fruits of ecumenism were that Orthodox Christians became more honest in speaking to others in ecumenical settings about Orthodox faith and life, and more earnest about putting their theology and ecclesiology into practice, these two things alone would justify Orthodox participation in ecumenism.

The Duty of Ecumenism

A conviction that Orthodox Christians must be involved in ecumenism does not preclude discernment. Orthodox may for various reasons decide not to participate in certain ecumenical organizations or movements, or they may decide to change their manner of participation. Orthodox even may decide not to work ecumenically with some non-Orthodox churches and movements.[11] For practical reasons, some Orthodox churches may find it impossible to participate in formal ecumenism at all. But certainly Orthodox churches, in accordance with

[10]Cf. *The Unity We Still Seek* and *Confessing the One Faith* in this present volume.

[11]See Fr John Reeves, "The Price of Ecumenism," where he advocates "a new approach to ventures ecumenical" for Orthodox, Roman Catholics, and conservative evangelicals that hopefully can avoid "the chief architectural flaws of the old Protestant-style ecumenical movement."

the gospel of Jesus Christ, are obliged to work in whatever ways the Lord provides to meet and cooperate with non-Orthodox Christians, and indeed with all people, for the sake of whatever is true, honorable, just, pure, lovely, gracious, excellent, and worthy of praise. (Phil 4.8) They are especially obliged to work with separated Christians, of whatever sort and whatever spirit, to clarify disagreements, overcome divisions, build up unity in God and in Christ, and collaborate in doing good deeds for human beings, especially those who suffer.

Doing these blessed duties is what ecumenism, rightly understood, is about. Like all good things of God, it will be misunderstood and maligned and attacked, perhaps even by some, like those known to St Paul, whose "zeal is for God, but is not according to knowledge (*ou kat' epignosen*)," and who therefore "being ignorant of the righteousness that comes from God and seeking to establish a righteousness of their own . . . did not submit to the righteousness of God" (Rom 10.2–4). Whatever the case, God will judge us all.

As Orthodox struggle to find God's will in order to acquire a common mind on the divisive subject of ecumenism, for God's glory and the good of God's people, let each of us pray for the other in St Paul's words for those about whose "zeal for God" he bore witness: "Brethren, my heart's desire and prayer to God for them is that they may be saved" (Rom 10.1).

Orthodoxy in Post-Modern Pluralistic Societies[1]

"Democracy," said Winston Churchill, "is the worst form of government, except for all those other forms that have been tried from time to time."

I agree. As the grandson of Carpatho-Russian immigrants to the United States, I cannot imagine my life in any other society. I am extremely grateful for my personal destiny. But as an Orthodox Christian, blessed with higher learning, faith, family, priesthood, and theological education, I cannot imagine a way of life more insidious to Christian Orthodoxy and more potentially dangerous to human being and life than American liberal democracy.

"*Corruptio optimi pessima*: The corruption of the best is the worst." The most evil vice is always the perversion of the most excellent virtue. There is no better example of this than what has happened and continues to happen to American liberal democratic society, with its capitalist economics, its affirmation of human equality and individual rights, and its insistence on total freedom for all persons and communities in their "pursuit of happiness" qualified only by the imperative that the rights and freedoms of another are not to be denied or violated.

Liberal democracy in the United States today is not what it was in 1947 when Churchill made the well-known remark cited above. Much has changed. The form of society now produced and exported by the United States is not the kind of democracy that Churchill described. Fifty years ago the "American way of life" was indeed liberal, democratic, and capitalistic; but it was not genuinely "pluralistic": it was White, Western, and Christian, grounded in a biblical worldview primarily as understood by Protestants, and a biblical ethic that was held,

[1]This is a revision of paper given at an Inter-Orthodox Conference on Gospel and Cultures held in Ethiopia in 1996. It was published in its original form with other papers from the conference in *Orthodoxy and Cultures*, Ioan Sauca, Ed. (Geneva: WCC) 1996.

however tenuously or hypocritically, by the vast majority of the people. Nor was it "post-modern," that is, the secularized, politicized, subjectivized, and carnalized way of life that has resulted from the "deconstruction" of science, metaphysics, theology and art in our time.

Orthodox Christians in North America, Western Europe, sections of the Middle East, Australia and Japan already live, in varying degrees, in the new social, political, and economic post-modern pluralism whose origins lie in modern American liberal democracy. Those in Eastern Europe are on their way to it with an undeterred determination. And those in the so-called third world have already been affected by it in many complex ways.

A Totally New Reality

Some Orthodox will respond to this description of things by quoting the Preacher and insisting that there is really "nothing new under the sun" (Eccl 1.9). Indeed, birth and death, pleasure and pain, righteousness and sin, peace and war, and the changing of the seasons have always been and always will be. But wise people also know that the ways in which human beings experience, understand, and interpret these constant realities are constantly changing.

Others will say that Orthodox Christians in all times and all places are inevitably in the situation in which they find themselves today. The Orthodox, according to this view, have always been a minority within a minority—misunderstood, feared, ridiculed, rejected, and persecuted, "by spear or by sneer" as Dostoevsky once put it. This was so in the earliest church, they say, when the Orthodox were a small group within the "Jesus movement" surrounded by gnostics, legalists, and fundamentalists of various sorts, as evidenced in the canonical New Testament scriptures. This was true in the Constantinian age, when the Orthodox Fathers and saints usually departed this life defeated and dishonored, while heretics, apostates, and plain evildoers ruled the Christian empire. It was true under the Ottomans and in Holy Russia, not to mention the Marxist horror. And, it is true today. So, from this point of view, things were never really any different from what they are now.

Some Orthodox also want to compare our time to that of the early church when Christians were divided among themselves in a great variety of groups and movements, with massive confusion and controversy among themselves. They were under violent persecution from a world that was both highly religious and highly carnal yet fully united in its outrage against those who, in their "irrational" stubbornness, resolutely refused to place the crucified Jesus equally among the many religious and spiritual paths available to sensible, tolerant, and cultivated people.

But, there are radical differences today from all previous times. Orthodoxy is not a persecuted, minority faith among a plethora of other spiritual movements in a pagan empire whose faithful Christian members are freshly and fervently proclaiming Christ's gospel. Nor is Orthodoxy the established faith of a Christian empire, whose persecuted saints constantly struggle with heretics, apostates, and sinners, and, in times of theological and political controversy, often with each other. Nor is Orthodoxy a variety of ethnic communities under Muslim or Marxist domination. Nor is it, in the so-called "diaspora," simply a collection of Orthodox exiles in heterodox countries undergoing massive secularization, transformation, and change.

Though still a minority church riddled with massive inner confusions, fears, pretensions, and divisions resulting from its two-thousand-year odyssey through history, Orthodoxy, for the first time ever, finds itself in a "global village" whose diverse peoples are moving towards a way of life that has begun to dominate the planet. This is the liberal, democratic, capitalistic, post-modern—and post-Christian—pluralism that already reigns in what was once called the "first world."

From Modern to Post-Modern

Remnants of the old "modern" world remain in the United States today. They remain as well in the world that the United States is producing and for which it remains the ideal, no matter how much some may deny, deplore, and resist it. Religious toleration, racial equality, and minority rights, for example, are still issues of major concern in the United States and everywhere else in the world. The right to work, equal employment opportunities, safe working conditions, and a just wage are still sought and fought for in the economic arena. Universal education and health care, adequate housing, and compassionate immigration policies are still matters of critical social concern. In religious, philosophical, scientific, and artistic arenas, the old *modern*

issues (Descartes, Kant, Darwin, Newton, Freud, Marx . . .), such as the
relationship between faith and reason, science and theology, critical
thinking and fundamentalism, liberty and authority, individual conscience and traditional mores, even orthodoxy and heresy, continue to
attract passionate attention and concern. However, these issues are no
longer viewed and interpreted as they once were. In post-modern pluralistic societies they are seen in a whole new way, within a whole new
context, and with a whole new agenda for action.

This new universe of thought, discourse, and behavior is the direct
result of a modern, secular society's reduction of Christianity to a pri-
vatized, compartmentalized "religion." Alexander Schmemann's brilliant critique of this phenomenon can still be read with great profit,
especially in post-Marxist societies.[2] It is a transmutation of the
Judaeo-Christian worldview and experience far beyond anything even
remotely imagined by Georges Florovsky (among many others) in his
critique of heterodox "pseudomorphoses" of Orthodoxy.[3] In modern
secularized society, the language, structures, symbols and rites of classical, biblical Christianity remain, while their content and meaning are
radically altered. In the post-modern "deconstruction" of the modern
worldview—by way of radical personal and cultural existentialism, the
sexual revolution, the mystical quest, the politicization of theology
and ethics and the explosion of material and spiritual hedonism and
avarice—traditional language, structures, symbols, and rites are re-cre-
ated; their original content and meaning being replaced by a whole new
reconstruction of reality.

In the post-modern pluralistic world there is no objective truth,
right, good, or beauty which all human beings are created to discover,
know, and believe; to which they are called to conform in thought,
word, and deed; in which they are privileged to delight and rejoice; and
for which they are blessed to give glory and thanksgiving to God. There
is no such thing as objective meaning and purpose. There is rather a

[2]See A. Schmemann, For the Life of the World (Crestwood, N.Y.: St Vladimir's Seminary Press, 1963) and Church, World, Mission (Crestwood, N.Y.: St Vladimir's Seminary
Press, 1979).

[3]Florovsky first used the term "pseudomorphosis" in a paper on "The Ethos of the
Orthodox Church," presented at a WCC Faith and Order consultation in Kifissia, Greece,
in 1959 and subsequently reprinted in The Ecumenical Review 122, 183–198. It refers to
things—such as biblical verses and theological statements—that take on new and different meanings from what they originally meant, in new and different settings.

creation of reality, or, more accurately, many creations of a plethora of pseudo-realities, produced by the subjective wills of individuals, parties, and "interest groups" in the context of politics, power, self-creation, and permissiveness. The tenets of modern liberal democracy become objects of worship and ends in themselves in a politically charged, hedonist world. Freedom becomes license. Acquisition becomes a right. Differences are deified. And happiness understood as material and pseudo-spiritual pleasure becomes obligatory for all.

More than sixty years ago, H. Richard Niebuhr said that modern American liberal Protestantism taught "a God without wrath brings man without sin into a kingdom without judgment through the ministrations of a Christ without a cross."[4] I would propose that in the new age of post-modern pluralism "deities without sovereignty bring humanoids without dignity into lifestyles without responsibility through the exploitation of a god or goddess of one's own choice and making, without tragedy."

Anyone who considers this a frightful exaggeration should take a closer look at politics, economics, law, education, medicine, religion, entertainment, and art in the United States today—and then at recent developments in all countries and regions of the world.

Four Unacceptable Responses

Four possible responses to post-modern pluralism seem to me to be unacceptable for Orthodox Christians.

The first is to deny that "post-modern pluralism" exists and is rapidly growing throughout the world. To misread what is happening and to underestimate its impact would be fatal for Orthodoxy. Post-modern pluralism is here and, barring a revolution or catastrophe of unimaginable proportions, it is here to stay.

Second, it would be a fatal mistake for Orthodox Christians to think that they and their churches are somehow immune to post-modernism and untouched by its influence and power. We Orthodox are as infectable—and infected—as any, and as easily diseased and deluded. We only need by God's grace to see ourselves as we actually are, which our saints tell us is a miracle greater than raising the dead, to acknowledge that this is so. A psychiatrist has said "a great deal of intelligence

---

[4]H. Richard Niebuhr, *The Kingdom of God in America* (Chicago, Ill.: 1937) 193.

can be invested in ignorance when the need for illusion is deep."[5] These could be the words of an ascetical saint describing spiritual delusion. This warning applies to us Orthodox, whose need for illusions and delusions about ourselves, our churches, our histories, our neighbors, and our contemporary world seems very deep indeed.

Third, Orthodox Christians may be tempted to respond to post-modern pluralism by rejecting the contemporary world and taking refuge in a world of their own making. In doing so they yield to the very threat they are called to expose and to the very temptation they are called to resist. That indeed is what post-modernism would have us do—and would defend our right and reason for doing. We cannot create our own realities for our own purposes by subjective fiat. We must engage reality as it is, and take responsibility for it before God. We must live in the world that, by God's providence, is ours.

Fourth, Orthodox Christians may fall prey to the lie that the post-modern pluralistic worldview is a great new opportunity for human-kind, inherently consistent with traditional Orthodox views of freedom, personal dignity, cultural diversity, incarnational theology, and apophatic mystical theology, as well as our equally traditional (if sometimes facile and superficial) criticisms of "Western" rationalism, pietism, legalism, and moralism.

Orthodoxy and Post-Modernism

There are several things that Orthodox Christians can and must do in the face of the post-modern pluralistic worldview, particularly in soci-eties where it has already taken hold.

From the start, Orthodox Christians must compel themselves to put Christ, and only Christ and his gospel, at the center of their concerns, doing only that which "seems good to the Holy Spirit and us" accord-ing to the "mind of Christ." Evaluating the world in a conciliar man-ner, finding a common mind, and forging a common plan of action as Orthodox Christians is crucial not only to our witness as the Church but also to the very survival of the Church. This would be no mean achievement in a post-modern pluralistic world that constrains us to construct our own particular versions of reality and history on the basis of our own self-determined desires, interests, and needs.

[5]C.W. Socarides, *Homosexuality: A Freedom Too Far* (Phoenix, Az.: Adam Margrave Books, 1995) 234.

Conciliarity—which is not something that Orthodoxy *has*, but something that Orthodoxy *is*— demands more than sacrifice. It demands death. *"Unless a grain of wheat falls into the earth and dies, it remains just a single grain; but if it dies, it bears much fruit. Those who love their life lose it, and those who hate their life in this world will keep it for eternal life"* (Jn 12.24–25). This saying of the Lord applies as much to parishes, dioceses, local churches, and patriarchates as to individual persons. It is totally antithetical to the post-modern pluralistic view, which in the name of our rights and liberties commands us not merely to love our lives in this world, but to create and deify them, defending them against anyone and anything that would have us do otherwise. How ironic and unbearably painful it is to watch Orthodox Christians and churches betray Christ and the gospel, as well as their own real self-interests, in their captivation to the demonic deceit that God himself would have us love, protect, and defend "our own" at the expense not only of others but also of truth itself.

Orthodox Christians must once and for all abandon the lie that Christ's gospel allows the retention of all the riches and glories of their peculiar national cultures and identities, and the deceit that Orthodoxy itself requires this. Orthodox in modern and post-modern pluralistic societies have largely accepted and enacted these deceptions, which have led to our present, pathetic conditions. Orthodox Christians in North America and Western Europe are far along the way to losing both their faith and their culture by fusing them together and acting as if they were one and the same. And, Orthodox Christians in post-Marxist lands seem to have learned nothing from the experience of their brothers and sisters in the West.

According to Christ's gospel, the only way to save our lives (and everything in our lives worth saving), for everlasting life in God's kingdom is to deny, forsake, and even to *hate* all things in this world for the sake of Christ, the gospel, and the kingdom of God. It is to hate our families, nations, possessions, and cultures—and even our earthly ecclesiastical institutions—for the sake of the truth (cf. Lk 14.25–26). It is, to use St Paul's powerful words, to regard "whatever gains I had . . . as loss because of Christ" and "to suffer the loss of all things, and regard them as rubbish" because of "the surpassing value of knowing Christ Jesus my Lord" and being "found in him" (Phil 3.7–9). These are strong words. But they are true, and we violate them at our own risk. The good things in life, not our weaknesses and faults, are our greatest temptations, for they become our idols that cause us to distort reality, deny truth, and endorse deception in our adoration of them.

In living solely according to the gospel of Christ, we must also resist the temptation to "hypostasize" Orthodoxy, to make it a "thing-in-itself," an ideology among ideologies, an instrument for furthering our national, political, cultural, or economic ambitions and desires. We must abandon what insightful critics of post-modern pluralism call "hyphenated" truths, values, histories, ethics, and art. We must never allow ourselves to speak of Orthodoxy, or of Orthodox theology, spirituality, culture and morality as if it were merely one among many choices and possibilities. We must rather speak from the perspective of the gospel and the Orthodox Christian tradition about *reality itself*, which is the same for everyone.

This point is critically important because the post-modern pluralistic worldview and rhetoric encourage the conviction that religions, movements, and cultures produce their own truths for themselves. They create their own ethics and art, and write their own histories according to their own interests and purposes. Post-modern etiquette regarding these "reality constructs" are basic: they are impervious to criticism from those outside their respective communities, but at the same time, they are to be endorsed as proper and legitimate for the community's members. But Orthodox Christians must defend the conviction that there is no such thing as Orthodoxy constructed just for the Orthodox, any more than there is womanist history or homosexual art or Buddhist ethics or Muslim spirituality that has the right to remain unchallenged by those outside the respective community, while at the same time insisting that all others must necessarily endorse it as proper and legitimate to its community's members. Truth is for everyone. Values are for all people. All have a rightful place within history. All can delight in art. Spirituality exists for all to share. No person or entity has the right to remain closed, untouched by the questions and criticisms of others and the human community as a whole. All have the duty to be tested as to their value, veracity, and validity for all people. Orthodoxy is no exception to this rule. Orthodox Christians must be ready to be questioned and challenged, just as they claim the privilege, even the duty, to question and challenge others.

This leads to the very essence of Orthodoxy's witness in the world: the conviction that Jesus Christ is the Son and Word of the only true God. He alone is the Way, the Truth, and the Life of all people. He is God's very Wisdom and Power in the world. He is God's Image according to which all men and women are made. He is the Head, not only of the Church, but the Head over all things *(hyper panta)* through his death on the cross. He is the one in, for, and by whom all things *(ta panta)* exist. He is the one in whom all things *(ta panta)* hold together and consist.

Jesus of Nazareth is not one of many lights in the world. He is the Light of the world who enlightens all men and women who sit in lands of darkness and in the shadow of death. He is Life itself, confined to no one culture, tradition, or nation, unbound even by the Orthodox Church, which is "his body, the fullness of him who fills all and in all." He is God's beloved Son, the Son of God's love, and God who is Love itself.

Wherever truth is, Christ is there. Wherever wise people find their way, however imperfectly, he is their wisdom and way. Wherever power and beauty exist, he is their origin and end. And wherever there is love, he is its source, content and rule, its definitive bearer and revealer in the world, its final fulfillment, completion, and perfection forever. This is Orthodox Christianity, always and everywhere. It is the evangelical "word of the cross," which perhaps never in human history has seemed more scandalous and foolish than in the contemporary post-modern pluralistic world in which we now live.

Contrary to post-modern propaganda, these convictions would not necessarily lead to the imperialist domination of "Christo-fascists" who would use military, economic, or cultural means to compel others to accept their dogmas, ethics, and versions of history. This can happen, as it did in the past and does today. But the Orthodox saints— and indeed the saints of all times and places whom the Orthodox perceive as inspired by God—have always opposed this to the point of shedding their blood at the hands of their own authorities or at the hands of their enemies.

Whatever the case in past or present, Orthodox Christians should always be prepared to tolerate every error and evil, while unmasking its falsehood and rebuking its sin. And they must be ready as well, with real rejoicing and without reluctance or regret, to affirm "whatever is

true, whatever is honorable, whatever is just, whatever is pure, whatever is lovely, whatever is gracious," with anything "excellent" and
"worthy of praise," wherever and in whomever these divine realities
are found (Phil 4.8). Orthodox Christians must also be willing to exercise their privilege and duty to intercede before God and to stand as
advocates before his face on behalf of all who, wittingly or unwittingly,
have been led astray by the devil.

Another imperative for Orthodox Christians in post-modern pluralistic societies is the call to evangelize, witness, and serve all people
without discrimination, domination, or condition, and indeed without
even the desire to convert or reform—which is God's job, not theirs.
They are only to announce Christ's gospel, testify to the truth, serve
every person and be ready to suffer the consequences. Though this was
always the task of Orthodox Christians, they did not always fulfill it;
nor did their neighbors, whatever their convictions. In a world in which
those who claim to be in any way "orthodox" are suspected and
feared—sometimes, sadly, for many right reasons—this imperative is
especially crucial.

To be faithful to their calling, Orthodox Christians must be free and
respect the freedom of others, while proclaiming and proving that true
freedom is found only in knowing and doing the Truth. Perhaps no
ideal and no idol is more present and powerful in modern and post-
modern societies than freedom. And, perhaps nothing is more misunderstood, misused and abused. Democracy and Christianity inherently
demand freedom. American liberal democracy in its original form is
perhaps history's greatest proof of this principle, and imperial Russia,
perhaps, the most tragic example of its violation.

As long as the "American experiment" remained rooted in its
Christian soil, it served as an example of freedom in accordance with
the gospel message. It was, as Churchill said, the "worst form of government" except for all others. It deteriorated into its present condition by sin, by ceasing to be overtly Christian and by becoming an
idolized end-in-itself; so that every participant and group demanded
the right not only to be respected and tolerated, but to be affirmed and
approved without question or condition. It collapsed, and continues to
collapse, through the loss not only of basic Christian doctrine and
ethics, but also of the conviction that there is any objective truth and
righteousness for all people in any form whatever. Because of this, the

transformation of modern American liberal democracy into a post-modern pluralistic plethora of hostile and warring interest groups, including some that bear the name "Christian," was inevitable. So was its progression towards what Pope John Paul II has called a "culture of death."

Death, not life, is ultimately what post-modern pluralism is about. It is the essence of its ethos. We are speaking here not merely about the death of the mind and the spirit, but of the soul and body, and of human community and society itself. Dostoevsky revealed the roots of this madness in his literary exposure of "modernism." Metropolitan John of Pergamon analyzed it in his studies on being as communion and communion as truth.[6] Liberal democracy and free-market capitalism in its "deconstructed" post-modern forms are literally lethal. They cannot be otherwise. There is an ontological law at work here that cannot be violated except unto death. The "Kirillov" syndrome, artistically described by Dostoevsky in *The Demons,* and analyzed philosophically and theologically by Metropolitan John and others, is clearly demonstrated in an existential and historical way in contemporary modern and post-modern North American and Western European societies.

To see that this is so, one need only to examine "first-world" political, military, economic, and sexual practices; the activity of the media; contemporary entertainment and art; the handling of the AIDS crisis and abortion; and the euthanasia and "right-to-die" movements. What the way of "Kirillov" achieved for the modern alienated, libertarian individual, post-modern pluralists achieve for deconstructed and corrupted humankind as a whole. In its most radical and advanced expressions, the "culture of death" not only permits humans the right to demonstrate their freedom by spiritual and physical suicide, but it allows them the liberty to kill others as well.

Orthodox Christians must stand in the contemporary world not only by affirming life against death, but by affirming death in its true light, as the "final enemy" to be confronted, taken up and destroyed. We know that death is destroyed in Christ. It is destroyed not by life-affirming rhetoric, positive thinking and an upbeat attitude in the "pursuit of happiness." Still less is it overcome by political activity,

---

[6]John Zizioulas, *Being as Communion* (Crestwood, N.Y.: SVS Press) 1985.

legal action, economic development, sexual liberation, or the will to power. Even less is it achieved by military operations against select evildoers of one's choice. Nor is it conquered by the acquisition of possessions, properties, positions, profits, and prestige, however much we might allegedly desire all others to share in them as well. It is overcome, defeated, and destroyed only by truth, justice, and love fulfilled in self-sacrificial suffering. It is ultimately conquered solely by the refusal to resist evildoers, even unto death, in order to remain untouched by their evils.

The paschal proclamation of Christ's victory over death is Orthodoxy itself. The Lord conquers death by taking up sin, becoming a curse, embracing pain, enduring suffering, and being obedient to God the Father even unto death on the cross in unconditional love for sinners and by becoming their steadfast intercessor and advocate before God the Father. Christ's disciples are called to do nothing other than what their Master has done for the salvation of humanity and the whole of creation:

> God did not send the Son into the world to condemn the world, but in order that the world might be saved through him . . . And this is the judgment, that the light has come into the world, and people loved darkness rather than light because their deeds were evil . . . But those who do what is true come to the light, so that it may be clearly seen that their deeds have been done in God. (Jn 3.17,19,21)

The Narrow Way of Orthodoxy[1]

> . . . narrow is the way that leads to life, and few
> there be who find it. (Mt 7.14)

The holy Fathers teach us never to give advice unless we are asked. On this principle I could justify giving advice to you who live in lands formerly dominated by Communist regimes since you have asked me to speak to you. But I cannot be so bold. I have no advice to offer you. Rather I will share with you some of my convictions about Orthodox life in a democratic, pluralistic society. These convictions result from the experiences of two centuries of Orthodox Church history in North America. They derive most especially from our American experiences of the past seventy-five years, for more than thirty of which I have served as an Orthodox priest, pastor, and professor of theology.[2]

In sharing my convictions with you, I have no intention to teach you. I hope rather to stimulate your reflections by imitating the men described by St John Climacus who, while sinking in the mud, called out to others to warn them how they had got there. They did this so that those passing by would not fall in the same way (cf. *Ladder of Divine Ascent*, Step 26, 14). I pray that my words will be helpful.

"I Am a Christian"

When the early Christian martyrs were brought before their persecutors they often answered the threats of their torturers with the simple words: "I am a Christian!"

---

[1]This paper was originally read at a conference on "The Historical Road of Russian Orthodoxy, Yesterday and Today" in St Petersburg in 1993. It was also presented in adapted forms at conferences in Slovakia and Romania.

[2]I am preparing this paper for publication now after more than 40 years in the priesthood, having been ordained in 1963.

The first Christian believers had no earthly identity. They were dead to this world. They belonged to God's kingdom. In their homelands they were aliens. In foreign lands they were at home.[3] They belonged everywhere and nowhere, for they were "fellow citizens with the saints and members of the household of God" (Eph 2.19).

By virtue of their having been baptized into Christ and sealed with the Holy Spirit, thereby becoming participants in the eucharistic supper of God's coming kingdom, the believers in the Holy Trinity considered themselves as being dead to this world. Their lives were now "hid with Christ in God" (Col 3.3). They identified themselves, fundamentally and essentially, no longer as Greeks or Jews, slaves or freemen, barbarians or Scythians, or even as men and women (Galatians 3.27–28, Colossians 3.11). They were now *Christians*—"a chosen race, a royal priesthood, a holy nation, God's own people" (Acts 11.26, 1 Peter 2.9). Such was the spiritual consciousness of Orthodox Christians in the apostolic Church, the consciousness of the Church's saints throughout the ages. This was their deepest personal experience and their steadfast conviction as members of the one, holy, catholic, and apostolic Church of Christ.

This consciousness, experience, and conviction have to a large degree been lost by the great majority of Orthodox Christians now living in North America. How few there be—even among the bishops and priests—who have this fundamental, essential identity of being Orthodox Christians who belong to the one true Church which is, here and now, the foretaste of God's kingdom to come for peoples of all nations of the earth.

For the most part, we Orthodox in North America view our church membership primarily in terms of our ancestry. We are Arabs from various countries, or Albanians, Bulgarians, Carpatho-Russians, Greeks, Macedonians, Romanians, Russians, Serbians, Ukrainians—and our churches are mostly identified in these ways. If we are converts, we

[3]Letter from a Christian disciple to Diogenetus (2nd century): "Christians are not distinguished from the rest of humanity by either country, speech, or customs. They do not live in cities of their own; they use no peculiar language, they do not follow an eccentric manner of life. They reside in countries (with the rest of us) but only as alien citizens. They obey the established laws, but in their own lives they go beyond the law. In a word: what the soul is in the body, the Christians are in the world. The soul dwells in the body, but does not belong to the body; just so Christians live in the world, but are not of the world . . . Every country is their homeland, and every homeland, a foreign country."

belong to churches identified in one or another of these ways. And, however we may view ourselves, Orthodox in the Old World look upon us in this way and almost without exception consider us to be an ecclesiastical "diaspora"—no matter how long we have been living in the United States or Canada, often as citizens of these countries, and despite the fact we have been worshipping in Orthodox churches that have been here for centuries.

We in the United States and Canada are divided into many ecclesiastical "jurisdictions" on the basis of nationality, ethnicity, and political ideology. We claim that we are one and the same Orthodox Church, and in liturgical rites and creedal statements we are. But we openly and shamelessly use our ecclesiastical structures for nationalistic, cultural, ethnic, and ideological ends. We employ our church buildings as shrines of national heritages, museums for cultural exhibitions, concert halls for ethnic performances, training centers for languages and customs, and meeting places for patriotic and political programs and activities. We are free to do so. We have religious and political liberty. And it is, after all, primarily for this freedom that we or our parents and grandparents came here in the first place.

If we North Americans dislike what is being done in our churches, we are free to cross the road with like-minded people and open another church of our own; even one that we call "Orthodox." This has happened again and again. The result is ecclesiastical and spiritual chaos, disorder, hostility, competition, and opportunism with the Orthodox churches, with a steady decline in church membership in those without an ongoing immigration of Orthodox peoples from the "old countries." The result is an almost total loss of evangelistic and missionary consciousness and activity in all of the churches.

Except for a faithful few who strive to follow the narrow way which leads to life, we members of the Orthodox churches in North America have largely lost our basic identity and consciousness as Orthodox Christians. We do not identify ourselves first and foremost, not to say essentially and exclusively, as Christians—we are "Orthodox Christians" who also claim one or another ancestral nationality or heritage. And, we certainly do not organize and administer our church life on the sacred Orthodox principle that calls for unity and cooperation among all Orthodox believers living in the same—and related—territories and nations regardless of their nationality and ethnicity.

From 1794, when the Orthodox missionaries first came to Alaska, until the early decades of the twentieth century, Orthodox Christians in North America were in one unified church. But since that time, especially after the Bolshevik revolution, the North American missionary diocese of the Russian Orthodox Church splintered into many factions and groups. And, we Orthodox Christians exist in this disorderly and noncanonical manner to this day.

Recent events in your newly liberated countries fill some of us with sorrow and dread, for we see you sinking into the same "mud" in which we ourselves are stuck. Will there be Orthodox Christians among you who will follow the hard and narrow way of Christ which is uncompromisingly opposed to the broad and easy way of ecclesiastical division and schism because of nationalistic, ethnic, chauvinistic, political, ideological, and personal passions and interests? Will there be at least some, especially among the bishops and priests, who will resist the broad and easy way that leads to destruction, both here and in the age to come? Will there be at least some who say: "I am a Christian. I am Orthodox. I belong to the one, holy, catholic, and apostolic Church of Christ. I am of one mind, one heart, one soul, and one body with all those who belong to Christ and the Church, whatever their nationality and political opinions. I stand steadfastly opposed to those who use Christ's Church for any secular, nationalistic, ideological, or political purpose, however apparently noble and justifiable"?

The future of Orthodoxy depends on the few in all countries of the earth who follow the narrow way which leads to life, the narrow path that demands that the Orthodox Church be the Church of God and of Christ, and nothing but the Church: the presence and foretaste of God's kingdom on earth for all peoples who wish to enter and be saved.

Church and Society

The Orthodox Church is not of this world, but it is in the world for the sake of its salvation.

> For God has so loved the world that he gave his only begotten Son, that whoever believes in him should not perish, but have eternal life. For God sent his Son into the world, not to condemn the world, but that the world through him might be saved. (Jn 3.16–17)

The Lord Jesus Christ said that he is the Son of God who gives his flesh and blood "for the life of the world" (Jn 6.51).

The Orthodox Church can never be identified with this world. It is the presence of God's kingdom in this world until Christ comes again in glory at the end of the ages to establish God's kingdom throughout the whole of creation. But the Church is *in* the world for the sake *of* the world's life and salvation.

The narrow way that leads to life forbids Orthodox Christians to follow the destructive way of identifying Christ's Church with any particular social, political, economic, or military policy. It forbids anyone from using Christ's Church for any worldly purposes. But the narrow way that leads to life also forbids Orthodox Christians from taking the broad and easy way of withdrawal from direct involvement in the social, political, economic, and even military activities of the nations in which they live. It forbids them from taking the destructive way of turning Christ's Church into a self-enclosed, sectarian cult that has nothing to do with the world for which Christ was crucified and glorified, except to treat it with scorn and derision as something wicked which lies outside God's saving love and concern.

Orthodox bishops and priests, by virtue of their ordination and calling, may not hold worldly positions and participate directly in secular affairs. They may not serve in political offices, manage economic policies, or participate in military actions. Such activity is forbidden to the clergy by the Church's canons. But the Church's pastors and teachers are called to guide and direct Orthodox Christian laypeople in their calling to bring God's kingdom to every aspect of their daily life and work in the world by every possible means. The bishops and priests are called to instruct and inspire their believing people to make social, political, economic, and even military decisions and actions according to the teachings of Christ and the power of the Holy Spirit. They are called to urge their flock to do so freely, humbly and honestly, with love and respect for those with whom they disagree, both within the Church and outside her borders.

There is no infallible Orthodox Church teaching on social, political, economic and military policies. This is an area for legitimate differences of opinion among people of good will, including Orthodox Christians. But the narrow way of Christ compels Orthodox laypeople to be involved in life and work nationally, and internationally. It compels them neither to scorn the world which God loves and saves in his only-begotten Son Jesus Christ, nor to be swallowed up and consumed by the world to the point where the Church becomes nothing other than a tool for the worldly activities of impassioned and undisciplined people devoid of true Christian faith and spiritual life.

How well we in North America know the broad and easy ways that lead to the destruction, in both ecclesial and social life. How well we know the way of destructive sectarian withdrawal from the life of the world to the point where there is virtually no Christian witness and impact in social, political, economic, and military life at all. And, how well we know the opposite way of destructive immersion within the activities of the world, to the point where virtually all Christian witness and influence is lost. May the Lord preserve Orthodox Christians in the newly emerging democratic countries of Europe and Asia from falling into either of these destructive ways that we in North America know only too well.

Liturgy and Life

The Orthodox Church is essentially a worshipping Church. We glory in our liturgical life and devotion. We love our services and sacraments, our rites and rituals, our customs and traditions. Liturgical life and worship have preserved the Orthodox Church and the faith of countless Orthodox Christians in the darkest hours of Islamic oppression and Marxist persecution, as well as in the painful conditions of immigrant life in the capitalistic countries of the New World, where many Orthodox believers found themselves outside the mainstream of social, political, and economic power and privilege.

But destructive temptations, which are always distortions of what is godly and good, also confront Orthodox Christians as regards liturgical worship. On the one hand there is the broad and easy way of turning the Church's worship into a self-enclosed cult, providing an easy and comfortable escape from the life and activity of the world. On the other hand there is the equally broad and easy way of making the liturgy nothing but the decorative and sentimental expression of national and cultural traditions and interests. Such "worship" becomes devoid of any power to provide a critical engagement of God's kingdom with the real lives of those who attend and participate, and equally devoid of a critical judgment of God's truth upon their attitudes and actions in their daily activities. We in North America are well acquainted with both of these broad and easy ways that lead to destruction.

According to Christ's narrow way that leads to life, the Church's liturgy provides both a critical judgment on the world and a crucial empowerment of believers who must witness to Christ in their everyday lives. The Church's liturgical services and sacraments enable and empower believers to experience here and now the truth and beauty of God's kingdom. They allow them already now to experience the "righteousness and peace and joy in the Holy Spirit" which, according to the apostle Paul, "the kingdom of God is" (Rom 14.17).

In order to be what it is, the Church's liturgy must be, as the liturgical service itself says, "reasonable worship, *logiki latreia*" (cf. the *anaphora* of the Divine Liturgy of St John Chrysostom). It must be accessible and meaningful to its participants. The Church's liturgy must be connected to the real lives and the real experiences of real people. It cannot be the ritualistic enactment of ancient rites performed in a perfunctory manner in languages that no one really understands, according to measurements of time which nobody observes, by ministers who have little, if any, understanding or interest in the content of what they are doing and why. The Church's sacraments and services cannot be "mysteries" in the sense that they are mystifying, meaningless, and nonsensical to those who perform and participate in them in quasi-magical and mechanical ways; nor can their meaning be determined by subjective personal, religious, cultural, ideological, and/or political purposes.

Our experience in North America proves that the Church's liturgy is truly the presence of God's kingdom on earth for those who seek and desire Christ's narrow way that leads to life. For those who believe in the Holy Trinity and desire "reasonable worship," the Orthodox liturgy is truly divine. Radical revision or substantial reformation of its form and content are unnecessary. But the liturgy is in need of continual spiritual attention and practical updating regarding its external forms, such as styles of chanting and ritual and language, so that it may always be what it divinely is: the living experience of God's kingdom for the faithful in the midst of the earth.

Our American experience demonstrates clearly that the Church's liturgy can be misused and abused. It can be frozen and fossilized. It can be nothing but a collection of irrelevant cultic rituals devoid of meaning, power and life. It can be the presence not of God's living kingdom in this present world, but the presence of a world long gone, the dead relic of a past time and place (usually somewhere in the nineteenth century, although some may prefer other bygone centuries). It can be a ritual in which what is of God and what is of merely human, sometimes mistaken, creation is indistinguishable. When this occurs, people go to the church building as they go to a museum or theater: to see what people of another age looked like, how they spoke and sang, how they dressed and behaved. And, if they so choose (for any number of reasons), they can themselves imitate their actions. What happens in such cases, which are all-too-familiar to Americans, is that the Church's services and sacraments have little or nothing to do with present-day life in our contemporary world. Regrettably, for some who choose this broad and easy way, the less the Church's liturgy has to do with contemporary reality the better. The stranger and less understood and less accessible the liturgy is to normal people, the "more mystical" and "more Orthodox" it is considered to be.

Societies steeped in religious liberty are especially prone to producing massive variations in liturgical attitudes and practices that do not express the rich and positive diversity inspired by God's Holy Spirit in the Church. These differences in practice are rather the sinful expressions of human ignorance, opinion, and passion. The churches in the United States and Canada have suffered from these distortions. We pray that you be spared this experience in your newly emerging countries, but we fear that many human beings (being what they are) will be tempted to abandon the narrow way that leads to life.

May the Lord grant that the liturgical services and sacraments of the Orthodox churches in the new countries of Europe and Asia be the true worship of God in spirit and truth, brought to the world by Jesus Christ and preserved in the Church by the Holy Spirit. God grant that Orthodox worship in these lands be according to Christ's narrow way which leads to life. May it not be the broad and easy way of re-enactment of external forms and cultic rituals, disconnected from the real lives of real people, which leads to the destruction of people's lives, especially the majority of young people who expect the Church to have something directly to do with their spiritual aspirations, desires, and needs.

And, speaking of the youth, our experience has been that liturgical worship without catechetical instruction and the possibility to participate directly in Christian work and spiritual life produces no long-lasting fruits of the Holy Spirit; neither does catechetical instruction and participation in activities that are disconnected from well-prepared participation in the Church's liturgical life experienced as "reasonable worship."

Orthodox and Heterodox, Believers and Non-believers

Our experience in the United States and Canada, especially in recent years, has also revealed that on either side of Christ's narrow way concerning the relationship between Orthodox Christians and non-Orthodox, and between believers and non-believers, there exist two broad and easy ways, opposite to each other and equally pernicious and destructive.

One broad and easy way is to consider everyone and everything outside the Orthodox Church to be totally devoid of God's grace and goodness, totally untrue and totally evil. Those on this path consider Roman Catholic and Protestant Christians, as well as members of the pre-Chalcedonian Oriental churches (the Egyptian Copts, the Armenians, the Ethiopians, and the Syrian Christians of India) as not being Christians at all. They hold that their services and sacraments are wholly devoid of grace and truth, that there is nothing of God and the true Church of God in their doctrines and practices. They consider "ecumenism" to be heretically sinful, even when "ecumenism" is understood as all Orthodox Churches in the world today officially understand it, namely, as the work to overcome disagreements and divisions among Christians and Christian confessions and communities, to affirm unanimities and agreements where these actually exist, and to cooperate in practical activities whenever possible for the good of human beings, especially the poor, needy, afflicted, outcast, and suffering. Those following this way decry discussion or cooperation; they only condemn and judge others, and they justify this as Orthodox strictness, as the narrow way itself!

The opposite broad and easy way, also well-known in the United States and Canada, is to consider all Christian confessions and communities, and perhaps even all religious philosophies and movements, as essentially the same, or at least not significantly different enough to be a matter of importance. Those on this destructive path view Orthodoxy as the cultural religious expression of the traditionally Orthodox peoples that is to be rigorously preserved by these nations for themselves. They see no need for any theological dialogue with others, and no need for any missionary activity. Cooperation might be welcome only if it serves the interests of the Orthodox.

The narrow way of Orthodoxy, however, rejects both of these destructive, false ways. Orthodox Christians have always insisted that the God of Abraham, Isaac, Jacob, Moses, and all the patriarchs and prophets of Israel is the only true God. We have always insisted that Jesus Christ is the Only-begotten Son and Word and Image of this one true God, who is his eternal Father. We have always held that Christ alone is the Way, the Truth, and the Life (Jn 14.6), and that the Holy Spirit alone is the Spirit of Truth (Jn 14.16; 15.26). We Orthodox have also always held that the Orthodox Church alone, among all Christian confessions and communities, is the one, holy, catholic and apostolic Church of Christ, "the household of God, which is the church of the living God, the pillar and bulwark of the truth" (1 Tim 3.15), Christ's very "body . . . the fullness of him who fills all in all" (Eph 1.23). Having participated for decades in "ecumenical activity," including membership on the Faith and Order Commission of the World Council of Churches, I have never heard one Orthodox Christian participant in North America or abroad ever deny any of these sacred truths.

But Orthodox Christians have also always held—and must continue to hold if we are true followers of Christ—that every human person is made in God's image and likeness, that virtually no human being is wholly devoid of God's grace and truth, that heterodox Christians and Christian confessions and communities do retain something of God and God's true Church, the so-called "vestiges of the Church" (vestigia ecclesiae) in their doctrines and practices, and that persons in these communities—not in spite of them but because of them—have sometimes attained extraordinary levels of righteousness and holiness. We Orthodox Christians also hold, according to the strict teachings of the Church's Holy Scriptures and tradition, including the witness of the saints, that non-Christians and even non-believers are not wholly devoid of God's grace and truth. Because of their being made in God's image and likeness, we can converse with them and cooperate with them and witness to them of Christ—and even learn some things from them—precisely on these bases.

The Orthodox Church is the one true Church of Christ who is the only saving Truth for human beings and the whole of creation. As such, the fully committed members of Christ's Church are given the grace to discern whatever is of God, and to rejoice and give thanks for it, wherever and in whomever it happens to be. We are also given the ability to discern what is not of the Lord, and to expose and reject it in the light of Christ, who is himself "the light of the world" (Jn 8.12), "the light which enlightens every person who comes into the world" (Jn 1.9).

The hard and narrow way of Christ, the way of Orthodox Christianity which leads to life, lies between the two wide and easy ways to destruction: the way of *religious sectarianism* on the one side, where we consider everything outside of the Orthodox Church to be nothing other than undifferentiated demonic darkness to be avoided at all costs; and the way of *religious relativism* on the other, where we would see no significant or substantial uniqueness in Orthodoxy, except for the fact that it is the traditional tribal religion of certain European, Middle Eastern, and Asian peoples—which is to be defended at all costs not only against those who would destroy it, but also against those who might wish to embrace it and accept it as their own.

We in the United States and Canada know these ways. Many are the sectarians and relativists among the members of the North American Orthodox Churches who follow these broad and easy ways. The pluralistic societies in which we live, in which there is such great and widespread spiritual conflict and complexity, provide a strong influence to surrender and succumb to one or the other of these two false paths. Happily, there are also the few who follow the hard and narrow way of Christ and the Church. These are they who affirm the absolute truth of the Orthodox Faith and the fullness of life of the Orthodox Church that empowers them with the freedom, honesty, and love to discern, affirm, and rejoice in the presence and power of the Holy Trinity both within and outside the boundaries of the one holy Church.

The Narrow Way of Orthodoxy

May Orthodox Christians throughout the world find and follow the
way of Christ and the Church, which is the hard and narrow way of
Orthodoxy. We can do so only by God's grace through remaining in
closest communion and cooperation with one another. There is no
infallible magisterium in Orthodoxy. No one person, bishop, or local
church possesses the whole truth on any given issue; and no individual, hierarch, or church community is exempt from error. The Orthodox Church is a *sobornal* church. It is a church in which the Holy Spirit
brings God's truth in Christ to the body of believers through the prayers
and spiritual feats of the saints. The Orthodox Church is a church in
which human persons discover God's truth by bearing each other's burdens, hearing each other's words, sharing each other's experiences, correcting each other's faults, and benefiting from each other's wisdom.

The religious, political and economic liberties that we now all enjoy,
and for which we give thanks, possess uniquely insidious forms of trial
and temptation. We in the United States and Canada know this from
long and painful experience. Our success in overcoming these temptations in uncompromising fidelity to the Lord has been minimal. Our
only hope is that there will always be the faithful few among us who
refuse to surrender to the broad and easy ways that lead to destruction.
May these trials and temptations, which are historically new for you,
and therefore especially enticing and attractive, prove to be as power-
less over true Orthodox believers as were the atheistic forces of the past
with their persecutions, imprisonments, and executions. May there
always be among you, as hopefully among us, those who remain steadfastly faithful to God.